Important Symbols

D1169074

Important Symbols
in
Their Hebrew, Pagan,
and
Christian Forms

Compiled by Adelaide S. Hall

Ibis Press
An Imprint of Nicolas-Hays, Inc.
Berwick, Maine

Puublished in 2003 by Ibis Press
An Imprint of Nicolas-Hays, Inc.
P. O. Box 1126
Berwick, ME 03901-1126
www.nicolashays.com

Distributed by Red Wheel/Weiser LLC
Box 612
York Beach, ME 03901-0612
www.redwheelweiser.com

Library of Congress Cataloging-in-Publication Data
Hall, Adelaide S. (Adelaide Susan), b. 1857
    [Glossary of important symbols in their Hebrew, pagan, and Christian forms]
    Important symbols in their Hebrew, pagan, and Christian forms / compiled by
    Adelaide S. Hall.
       p. cm.
    Originally published: A glossary of important symbols in their Hebrew, pagan, and
    Christian forms. Boston : Bates & Guild Co., 1912.
      Includes bibliographical references and index.
      ISBN 0-89254-074-5 (pbk. : alk. paper)
       1. Symbolism.   I. Title.
    BF1623.S9H35 2003
    302.2'223--dc21   2003045278

Typeset in Minion
Cover design by Daniel Brockman

Printed in the United States of America

VG

10 09 08 07 06 05 04 03
8 7 6 5 4 3 2 1

CONTENTS

Introduction

Each year, the stream of travel increases and many people are brought in contact with ancient terms and devices with which they are totally unfamiliar. Each year, new classes are formed in the History of Art and thousands of students enter art schools where they copy classic designs which represented in the past the customs and beliefs of powerful and intelligent people.

In order to thoroughly enjoy historical and religious works or to interpret the exact language of form and color in ancient buildings, it is necessary to be acquainted with the most important emblems, from their origin in the past to the present application of these terms.

The Bible contains the largest number of symbols of any history in the world. Readers and teachers need to be familiar with the popular forms of expression employed by Hebrew, Pagan and Christian, in order to interpret correctly the Scriptures as well as classic and romantic literature.

Architects, sculptors, decorators and illustrators of fact and fiction, designers of book covers and plates, smiths and jewelers are often at a loss to find an object which will lend itself to their design and at the same time typify something or someone that they desire to suggest or memorialize in its plan.

The reasons governing the connection between the larger number of symbols and their meanings are so wrapped in myth and legend that an entire volume is often necessary to explain a few emblems. The greatest need seems to be—which are the important symbols and what do they signify.

Therefore, the compiler of this manual respectfully submits to all readers, travelers and students, a list of symbols culled from her collection of notes covering a period of nine years' study upon the subject and an equal number of trips abroad. In the majority of cases the emblem has been personally verified. Also, a selected bibliography of helpful books for those who desire to make a study of the subject. All of these works may be found either in the libraries of Boston or of Chicago.

ADELAIDE S. HALL

EXAMPLES

Medium	*Place*
Architecture and Sculpture.	Temples of Egypt, India, China and Japan. Cathedrals and other early churches of Europe. Monuments. Tombs. Ornaments. Amulets.
Painting.	Tomb decorations in Egypt and India. Kakemonos or wall hangings in China and Japan. Frescoes, easel pictures and illuminated manuscript. Stained glass windows. Heraldic shields and banners. Porcelain and pottery in folk lore designs.
Weavings and Embroideries.	Tapestry from Babylonian times to the present; rugs, carpets, brocades, tissues, and garments.
Crafts work in chiseling, incising and carving.	Coins, medals, seals, ornaments, altar ware, table ware, and jewelry.

TREES

"The festival of the Christmas tree is the survival of tree worship among the Germans. The first care of the missionaries was to cut down the groves of the pagans and to consecrate the spot by the erection of a chapel. One of the last vestiges of a grove is the tree 'Stock am Eisen' in Vienna."—*Fergusson.*

The ancients attached the utmost importance to the significance of trees, their poetic and impressive language. We find this when we read the Scriptures, look at our oriental rugs, or examine a Gothic cathedral.

Country	Symbol	Signification
	HEBREW AND PAGAN FORM	
	THE TREE OF LIFE OR UNIVERSE TREE	
EGYPTIAN	Date Palm	1. Life in the abstract.
		2. Residence of the gods.
ASSYRIAN	Pine Seven budded, seven branched.	Completeness.
CHALDEAN	Date Palm	Food for the soul.
SCANDINAVIAN	Ash "Yggdrasil"	Meeting place of the gods.
INDIAN	Pine	Fertility.
ZOROASTRIAN	Cypress	Emblem of Ormuzd, Creator of light.
GERMAN	Wishing Thorn	Divine succor and guidance.
	RESIDENCE TREES (CONVENTIONAL AND NATURAL)	
EGYPTIAN	Sycamore	1. Residence of Hathor as goddess of the West.
		2. Residence of Nut, Goddess of creative power.
	Acacia Tamarisk	Residence of Osiris, god of the sun.
PHOENICIAN	Cypress	Astarte, goddess of virility.
CASHMERE	Five trees of the Garden of Indra	Ambrosial sap for the gods.

Country	Symbol	Signification
RESIDENCE TREES—CONTINUED		
PERSIAN	Cypress	Residence of Mithra. Emblem of Zoroaster. Sovereign power.
BABYLONIAN	Palm	Residence of Istar, the divine mother.
GRECIAN	Willow	Birthplace of Hera, divine mother.
ROMAN	Myrrh	Birthplace of Adonis, god of beauty.
JAPANESE	Icho or Gingko tree	Sacred emblem of the gods: Eternal life.
GEM BEARING TREES OF PARADISE		
EGYPTIAN	Golden Sycamore of gem fruits and flowers	Sacred to Nut as goddess of the sky.
EAST INDIAN	Gem bearing tree	Sacred to Buddha.
CHINESE	Pearl bearing tree of Paradise	Purity in eternity.
ASSYRIAN	Luminous gem bearing tree	The Great Light of the god.
TREE OF HAPPINESS		
MOHAMMEDAN	Bearing all manner of fruits	Paradise: Joys of the Tooba.
CALENDAR TREE		
CHINESE	"Ming Kap" or Monthly tree. Fifteen buds on right of central stem and fifteen on left; one falls daily	Time's flight.
THE PINE TREE		
EGYPTIAN AND ASSYRIAN	Natural form	Symbolic tree of the gods.
CHINESE		Longevity.
JAPANESE		Longevity: Emblematic of spirits of Takasago and Suminoye. Conjugal affection and long life.

Country	Symbol	Signification
THE OAK		
JUDEAN	Natural form	Place of angelic visions. Emblem of Abraham.
GRECIAN		Emblem of Zeus, the father god. Majesty. The tree mother of the race. Emblem of Dodona grove, the seat of the Oracle.
ROMAN		Emblem of Jupiter, the father god. Majesty.
EARLY BRITISH		Sacred wood of Druidical altar.
THE ASH		
SCANDINAVIAN	Natural form	Emblem of Odin, the father god. Sovereignty. In connection with the elm they signify creators of the race.
NORTH AMERI-CAN INDIAN		Veneration of a nature god.
THE PLANE TREE		
GRECIAN	Natural form	Emblem of Xerxes. Love of Nature.
THE OLIVE		
GRECIAN	Natural form	Emblem of Athena, patron goddess of warriors. Symbol of victory.
ROMAN		Symbol of peace.
THE POMEGRANATE		
ROMAN	Natural form	Emblem of reproduction.
THE CEDAR		
JUDEAN	Natural form	Incorruptibility.
GRECIAN		Emblem of Artemis, goddess of the moon and of the chase.
EAST INDIAN		Fertility.
CHINESE		Fidelity.

Country	Symbol	Signification
THE LAUREL		
GRECIAN	Natural form	Inspiration.
ROMAN		Emblem of Apollo: Poetry. Antidote of evil eye: emblem of Daphne who was changed to a laurel to escape Apollo.
THE PIPPALA OR BO TREE		
EAST INDIAN, CHINESE AND JAPANESE	Natural form	Emblem of Buddha, under which he received perfect wisdom.
THE BAMBOO		
CHINESE AND JAPANESE	Natural form	Longevity.
THE PLUM		
JAPANESE	Natural form	Emblem of woman's purity. "Nightingale Dwelling Plum Tree," the emblem of daughter of Kino Tsurayuki or a sacrifice rewarded.
EARLY CHRISTIAN AND MODERN FORM		
IN GENERAL	Palm	Martyrdom to attain Heaven. Victory over the flesh. Righteous Christian.
	Fig	Fruitfulness. Good works.
	Oak	Majesty. Strength and endurance.
	Cedar	The Lord's tree. Emblem of Lebanon.
	Willow	Abandoned. Desperation and grief.
	Apple	Productiveness. The first sin. Emblem of Eve.
	Poplar	Sympathy. Tremulousness. Lamentation.
	Acacia	Friendship.
	Aspen	Emblem of Judas: fear.

Country	Symbol	Signification
	EARLY CHRISTIAN AND MODERN FORM—CONTINUED	
IN GENERAL	Christian tree of Life	Knowledge of good and evil. Tree of Eden. Tree of St. John's vision, bearing twelve manner of fruits for the healing of the nations. Golden tree of Galahad.
	Tree of Jesse	The human line or genealogical tree of Jesus.
	Holly	Holy tree. Emblem of Christmas festivities.
	Maple	Symbol of Canada.

EMBLEMS OF LIGHT
(Natural and Fictitious)

Since the words "Let there be Light" animated the Universe, light has been its most cherished possession. It has been venerated by the ancients by its emblems, the sun, moon and stars. Candidates for religious promotion were often kept in darkness for a period of time before being permitted to enjoy the light of the higher plane or office. The Japanese believe that no offering is ever so precious to Buddha as a lamp or a lantern and love to tell a story about their "Hall of the Lamps" on Mt. Koyasan. It contains ten thousand lamps, which are mainly votive offerings of the rich. One day a storm extinguished all the lights but one, that of a poor widow whose piety had led her to expend for this lamp, the few coppers she possessed. Today, we Christians symbolize our Saviour as the Light of the World.

Country	Symbol	Signification
	HEBREW AND PAGAN FORM	
	THE SUN	
IN GENERAL	Usual form	The active power of nature.
EGYPTIAN		Emblem of Osiris. Ra. Sovereignty.
ASSYRIAN		Emblem of Assur. Sovereignty.
PHOENICIAN		Emblem of Baal. Power—Might.
AMMONITES		Emblem of Moloch. Fierceness of sun's heat.
EARLY PERSIAN		Emblem of Mithra. Creation of light.
SCANDINAVIAN		Emblem of Loki. Blessing, fertility.
GRECIAN		Emblem of Helios, the light of the universe.
ROMAN		Emblem of Apollo as light of divinity.
JAPANESE		National emblem of Amaterasu as sun goddess and ancestress of the only dynasty. Emblem of the Emperor as a ruler by divine right.

Country	Symbol	Signification
		THE DAWN
HINDU	Usual form	Emblem of Ushas. Blessing. The bride.
GRECIAN		Emblem of Eos: youth: purity.
ROMAN		Emblem of Aurora as delicate beauty. Freshness.
		THE MOON
IN GENERAL	Usual form	The passive form of nature. When in crescent form signifies virginity.
EGYPTIAN		Emblem of Thoth, god of truth. Hathor, goddess of beauty.
JUDEAN		Emblem of Ashtaroth, goddess of fertility.
SYRIAN		Emblem of Astarte, goddess of material desire and heartlessness.
GRECIAN		Emblem of Selene as serene loveliness.
ROMAN		Emblem of Diana: goddess of the chase: chastity.
CHINESE		Heaven's beauty.
JAPANESE		Emblem of Susano-o: The seed of the siesta (because of previous night watching).
EARLY MEXICAN		Emblem of Metzli goddess of agriculture.
		THE STARS
ZODIACAL	Orion	Hunter of beasts.
	Gemini	Emblems of Castor and Pollux. Emblems of brotherly love.
MASONIC	Rayed star in a circle	Guidance.

Country	Symbol	Signification
THE STARS—CONTINUED		
GRECIAN	1. Alcyone, a single star	River of Heaven.
	2. A group of seven stars called the Pleiades	Opening of navigation.
	3. Group called the Hyades	Tearfulness.
MOHAMMEDAN	Six pointed star formed of two triangles	Emblem of the faith.
	Eight pointed star formed of two squares	Emblem of the faith.
THE MILKY WAY		
SCANDINAVIAN	Usual form	Pathway to Valhalla, the home of the gods.
NORTH AMERI-CAN INDIAN		Pathway of ghosts.
THE RAINBOW		
CHINESE AND JAPANESE	Usual form	Bridge of heaven.
THE TORCH		
HINDU GRECIAN	Usual form	Active power of nature. Progress.
FIRE		
JUDEAN AND HINDU	Altar fires	Sacrifice: consecration.
IN GENERAL	Beacon fires	Communication between men.
	Hearth fires	Home. Loyalty to family.
	Usual form	Votive offerings to the gods.
	Lantern and dragon	Emblem of Persian Sibyl, who prophesied overcoming evil by good.
TAPER OR CANDLE		
IN GENERAL	Usual form	Emblem of Libyan Sibyl, who prophesied the sight of the Saviour.

Country	Symbol	Signification
EARLY CHRISTIAN AND MODERN FORM		
THE SUN		
IN GENERAL	Usual form	Emblem of beneficence and fruitfulness.
	When illuminating a woman with the moon under her feet and crowned with stars	Emblem of Virgin Mary as overcoming the world. The spirit warring against the flesh.
THE MOON		
IN GENERAL	Usual form	Serene beauty. Pensiveness.
THE STARS		
IN GENERAL	1. The morning star 2. Star in the East 3. Cloud of stars	Reward of "He that overcometh." Emblem of the nativity. Infinitude.
THE RAINBOW		
IN GENERAL	Usual form	Promise.
THE TORCH		
IN GENERAL	Burning	Christ as the Light of the World.
	In hand	Emblem of St. Theodore.
LAMP		
IN GENERAL	Seven lamps or seven branched candlestick	Sacrament. Consecration. The seven primitive churches.
	Five lamps burning	The five wise virgins.
	Five lamps extinct	The five foolish virgins.
ENGLISH	Altar candle	One on each side of cross.
	Paschal candle (Passover)	On gospel side of choir.
	Processional candle	Carried in procession as the Head.

COLORS

"The men of primeval times did not see colors: only strong colors are seen by a child. No color has any symbolic meaning taken in itself, but only through association."

—*F. Delitzach, D.D.*

Country	Symbol	Signification
	HEBREW AND PAGAN FORM	
EGYPTIAN	White	Color of Osiris as judge of the dead. Mourning.
	Green	Material decay. Victory.
	Gold	Color of Horus as glory of the gods.
	Red	Color of good Genii. Representing virility.
	Black	Color of evil Genii. Representing destruction.
EAST INDIAN	Green	Emblem of Ganesa, god of widsom.
	Red	Color of Vishnu. Human love.
	Blue	Color of Krishna. Joyousness.
	Combination of red, blue and white	Emblem of Buddhistic trinity. Signifying intelligence, order and unity.
	Black or Blue	Antidote for Evil Eye. (Or envy.)
EARLY PERSIAN	White, red and gold	Emblem of Persian trinity signifying purity, love and revelation.
MOHAMMEDAN	Red	Spiritual beauty.
	Green	Knowledge of Allah.
GRECIAN	White	Color of Zeus as divine purity.
	Purple	Emblem of the Mysteries. Royalty. Secrecy.
	Red	Emblem of Spartans, who were courageous unto death.

Country	Symbol	Signification
COLORS—CONTINUED		
IN GENERAL	Red and black	From life to death.
	Green	Youth. Victory.
ROMAN	Red	Emblem of Bacchus, god of vigor and wine. Attribute of Pollux, as immortality.
	Purple	Royalty. Noble birth, as "born to the purple."
	Black	Attribute of Castor, as mortality.
	White	Emblem of Jupiter as chief divinity.
PLANETARY COLORS		
CHALDEAN	Golden yellow	Emblem of the sun.
	Black	Emblem of the moon.
	Orange	Emblem of Planet Jupiter.
	Red	Emblem of Planet Mars.
	Pale yellow	Emblem of Planet Venus.
	Blue	Emblem of Planet Mercury.
HUNGARIAN	Red Path	Emblem of Attila's blood stained trail.
CHINESE	Black	Emblem of the North. Water.
	Yellow	Emblem of the South. Color of the T'sing dynasty.
	White	Emblem of the West. Metal.
	Green	Emblem of the East. Wood.
	Red	The earth.
JAPANESE	Warm colors such as red, purple, orange, etc.	Masculine colors.
	Cold colors such as blue, pale yellow, grey, etc.	Feminine colors.
	White	Emblem of Minamoto clan.
	Red	Emblem of Taira clan.

Country	Symbol	Signification
	EARLY CHRISTIAN AND MODERN FORM	
IN GENERAL	White	The Creator. Perfection. Peace. Insignia of the imperial party of Italy—the Ghibellines.
	Blue	Heavenly truth. Sanctification.
	Red	Divine zeal. Creative force. Love of God.
	Purple	Dignity. Mourning.
	Purple-red	Severity.
	Purple-blue	Tranquillity.
	Green	Eternal youth. Hope. Victory over the flesh.
	Gold	Worth. Virtue. Glory of God. Christian might.
	Bright yellow	Fruitfulness. Beneficence. Truth.
	Dull yellow	Deceitfulness.
	Black	Penitence. The Papal party of Italy or the Guelphs.
	Violet	Humility. Suffering. Sympathy. Fasting.
	ANCIENT ACADEMIC GARMENT COLORS	
IN GENERAL	Blue	Philosophy.
	Black	Theology.
	Scarlet	Jurisprudence.
	Green	Medicine.
	Red	Emblem of executioner. War. Human love. High spirits.
	Vermilion	Spiritual purity.
	Scarlet (In Biblical sense)	Immorality.
	Black	Mourning.

Country	Symbol	Signification
ANCIENT ACADEMIC GARMENT COLORS—CONTINUED		
IN GENERAL	Green	Jealousy. Envy.
	Gold	Prosperity.
	Yellow	Bombast. Deceit.
HERALDIC COLORS		
ENGLISH	Sable or black	Grief. Penitence.
	Argent or white or silver	Purity. Faith.
	Gules or red	Courage. Zeal.
	Azure or blue	Sincerity. Piety.
	Vert or green	Hope. Youth.
	Purpure or purple	Rank.
	Tenné or orange	Endurance.
	Sanguine or blood red	Patriotism. Sacrifice.

NUMBERS

"Egyptian gods—the ordinary student may confine himself to the study of the divinities, important enough to have made in stone, bronze or pottery rather than those simply sketched upon the walls or mentioned in the inscriptions. Many names refer to the same divinity, called by different names in different localities. In China there are 57 sects all teaching the Christian religion to the natives; all different, yet the same spirit. The Moslems have 99 names for Allah."—*R. H. Blanchard.*

A Gnostic was a member of one of several sects which existed between the first and sixth centuries after Christ. They combined in their belief oriental theology, Greek philosophy and the doctrines of Christianity.

Country	Symbol	Signification
	HEBREW AND PAGAN FORM	
	THE MYSTIC NUMBER THREE	
MEMPHIAN	The Triad (3) Godhead	These are Ptah, Sekhet, Nefer-Tem.
THEBAN	Triad Godhead	Amem-Ra, Maut, Khonsu.
ABYDAN	Triad Godhead	Osiris, Isis, Horus.
HINDU	Triad Godhead	Brahma, Vishnu, Siva.
EAST INDIAN, CHINESE AND JAPANESE	Triad of Buddha	Personality, church, law.
IN GENERAL	The Triscula or Triskele	Which are three curves joined together, each by one end and forming a three spoked wheel, representing fertility.
SCANDINAVIAN	Triad Godhead	Odin, Thor, Frey.
SICILIAN	The Trinacria or three legs joined at thighs by the head of Medusa	Emblem of City of Palermo.
MANX	The three legs of the Isle of Man joined at the thighs	Emblem of Island.
GRECIAN	Three pointed trident or spear	Emblem of Poseidon, god of the sea.

Country	Symbol	Signification
GRECIAN	Three sickles of Megara	Good fortune.
ROMAN	Trident	Emblem of Neptune, god of the ocean.
	Groups of three	The Fates. The Furies. The Graces.
EARLY PERSIAN	Three fires	Anaid, fire of the stars. Mihr, fire of the sun. Berisov, fire of the lightning.

NUMBER FOUR

Country	Symbol	Signification
EGYPTIAN	Gods of the four winds	Ram-headed Qebui, the north wind, leopard-headed Shehbui, the south wind, ram-headed Henkhisesui, the east wind, asp-headed Hutchaiui, the west wind.
MOHAMMEDAN	Four fundamental duties	Prayer, alms giving, fasting, pilgrimage to Mecca.
JAPANESE	Four deva kings	Guardians of the Temple.

NUMBER FIVE

Country	Symbol	Signification
EAST INDIAN	Five powers of Brahma	Ether, air, fire, water, earth.
CHINESE AND JAPANESE	Groups of five	The five Buddhas, five (or multiple) Bodisatvas, or disciples of a Buddha.

NUMBER SEVEN

Country	Symbol	Signification
CHINESE	Seven days of Creation	Day of the fowl, dog, pig, sheep, cow, horse, mankind.
PERSIAN	Seven steps	Progress toward Heaven.
HINDU	Seven mansions	Abode of created spirits.
JUDEAN	Seven days	Fasting, sacrifice and prayer.
ROMAN	Seven planets	Sun, Moon, Mars, Mercury, Saturn, Jupiter, Venus.
GNOSTIC	The seven Greek vowels arranged in cabalistic manner to signify	The Creator.

Country	Symbol	Signification
JAPANESE	Seven household gods	Daikoku, the god of wealth. Ebisu, the god of fish and labor. Hotei, the god of contentment. Bishamon, the god of war. Fukurokuju, the god of longevity. Benten, the goddess of love. Juro-jin, the god of wisdom.

Number Eight

EGYPTIAN	Eight oared boat	The Tchetetfet of the Elysian fields or Heaven.
EAST INDIAN	The eight sacred myths. Eight elementary gods	Mystery of the faith.
GRECIAN	Eight gods of the wind	Boreas of the north, Kaekias of the northeast, Apeliotes of the east, Euros of the southeast, Notos of the south, Lips of the southwest, Zephyr of the west.
EAST INDIAN, CHINESE AND JAPANESE	The eightfold path of Buddha	Right faith, right resolve, right speech, right action, right living, right effort, right thought, right self-concentration.

Number Nine

GRECIAN AND ROMAN	Nine muses	1. Clio as muse of heroic endeavor, history. 2. Euterpe as Bacchanalian music; the flute. 3. Thalia as comedy. 4. Melpomone as song and tragedy. 5. Terpsichore as choral dance and song. 6. Erato as erotic poetry and the lyre. 7. Polyhymnia of inspired music.

Country	Symbol	Signification
	THE NINE MUSES—CONTINUED	
GRECIAN AND ROMAN	Nine muses	8. Urania of celestial phenomena. 9. Calliope of eloquence and epic poetry.
	NUMBER TEN	
ROMAN	The ten Sibyls or wise women	Prophecy.
	NUMBER TWELVE	
EAST INDIAN	Groups of twelve	Twelve orders of Dervishes.
JUDEAN	Groups of twelve	Sons of Jacob.
ROMAN	Groups of twelve	Tables of Roman law.
	NUMBER SIXTEEN	
CHINESE AND JAPANESE	Sixteen Arhats or disciples of Buddha	Nearing Nirvana or eternal bliss.
	NUMBER TWENTY-FOUR	
CHINESE	The twenty-four paragons.	Filial duty.
	NUMBER FIFTY-THREE	
JAPANESE	Refers to the fifty-three stations on the Tokaido or highway between Kyoto and Tokio	The way of the noble path of the empire.

EARLY CHRISTIAN AND MODERN FORM

Country	Symbol	Signification
	NUMBER TWO	
IN GENERAL	As opponent properties	Positive and negative. Warp and woof.
	NUMBER THREE	
IN GENERAL	Christian Triad-Godhead	Father, Son and Holy Ghost.
	NUMBER FOUR	
IN GENERAL	The four rivers	Tigris, Euphrates, Pison, Gihon.
	The four gospels	Matthew, Mark, Luke and John.
	The four winged beasts of the Apocolypse	The evangelists preceding.

Country	Symbol	Signification
NUMBER FIVE		
IN GENERAL	The five Patriarchates of the Greek Catholic church	Alexandria, Constantinople, Antioch, Jerusalem, Russia.
NUMBER SIX		
IN GENERAL	The number represents	The six attributes of the Creator which are Power, Majesty, Wisdom, Love, Mercy, Justice.
NUMBER SEVEN		
IN GENERAL	Seven stars	Angels of the seven churches which are Ephesus, Smyrna, Pergamus, Thyatira, Sardis, Philadelphia, Laodicea.
	Seven golden candlesticks	Emblem of the seven churches preceding.
	The number signifies	Completeness.
NUMBER NINE		
IN GENERAL	Usual form	The angelic number.
	The nine Worthies	These are of the Gentiles—Hector, Alexander, Julius Caesar. Of the Jews—Joshua, David, Judas Maccabeus. Of the Christians—King Arthur, Charlemagne, Godfrey of Bouillon.
	The nine fruits of the Spirit	Love, Joy, Peace, Long-suffering, Gentleness, Goodness, Faith, Meekness, Temperance.
NUMBER TWELVE		
IN GENERAL	The number signifies	The disciples of Christ. The pearls as the gates of the new Jerusalem.

Country	Symbol	Signification
	NUMBER TWENTY-FOUR	
IN GENERAL	The number signifies	The twenty-four elders of St. John's vision.
	NUMBER FORTY	
IN GENERAL	The number signifies	Fasting and prayer.
	NUMBER EIGHT HUNDRED AND EIGHTY-EIGHT	
SIBYLLINE	The number signifies "in 8 units 8 tens and 8 hundreds"	The name and nature of Christ.

ANIMALS

"The phonetic alphabets of the Phoenicians, Greeks and Romans were originally developed out of the primitive picture writing or hieroglyphics of the Egyptians. The system of an animal symbolism, which was such a prevalent feature of Christian art of the Middle Ages, was derived for the most part from an anonymous treatise on the nature of beasts, originally known by the name of Physiologus." (See *Ency. Britt.*) —*J. R. Allen, F. S. A.*

Country	Symbol	Signification
HEBREW AND PAGAN FORM		
THE LION		
EGYPTIAN	Natural form	Kingliness. Emblem of Sef or Yesterday and Tuau or Today.
	With human, animal or bird head	Emblem of deities or kings, denoting strength.
	Lion's head with globe and asp	Emblem of Tefnut, goddess of rain.
GRECIAN	Male lion	Majesty.
	Female lion	Protection.
	With breasts and head of a woman	Inscrutability. Pestilence.
ROMAN	Lion's skin	Emblem of Hercules, god of strength.
HEBREW	Leo	Zodiacal constellation denoting heat.
EAST INDIAN, CHINESE AND JAPANESE	With flaming tails	Guardians of Buddha's temples.
PERSIAN	Lion with sun	National emblem. Sun as residence of the Lion of Strength and Power.
THE TIGER		
CHINESE	Stars outlining tiger form	Constellation of the West and Autumn.

Country	Symbol	Signification
	THE TIGER—CONTINUED	
EAST INDIAN, CHINESE AND JAPANESE	Natural or conventional form	Materiality. The earth.
ROMAN	Tiger skin	Emblem of Bacchus as god of wine and revelry.
	THE IBIS	
EGYPTIAN	Either full form or head alone	Emblem of Thoth, god of truth, scribe of the dead.
	FOXES	
CHINESE	Natural form	Mischief, cunning.
JAPANESE	Conventional form	Emblem of Inari as goddess of rice as they are her messengers.
	THE LEOPARD	
IN GENERAL	Natural or conventional form	Stealthiness.
	THE BEAR	
RUSSIAN	Natural or conventional form	The friend of mankind.
	THE GOAT	
HEBREW	Stars outlining form	Zodiacal constellation of Capricorn.
SCANDINAVIAN	Natural form	Emblem of Thor as divine virility.
GRECIAN	Full form or horns and legs	Emblem of Pan, the nature god.
	THE DOG	
EAST INDIAN (Parsee)	Natural form	Vehicle of departing souls.
IN GENERAL	Natural form	Fidelity, obedience, science.
	THE CAT	
EGYPTIAN	Full form or head	Salacity. Emblem of Bast. Life giving rays of the sun.
	THE RAT	
CHINESE	Stars outlining rat	Zodiacal constellation.

Country	Symbol	Signification
	THE BULL	
HEBREW	Stars outlining form	Zodiacal constellation.
EGYPTIAN	Conventional or natural form with white triangle on forehead of black animal and twenty-eight other marks.	Emblem of Ptah as creative power.
EAST INDIAN, CHINESE AND JAPANESE	Conventional form	Reincarnation.
GNOSTIC	Natural form	Emblem of Ormuzd as creator of life.
	THE HORSE	
CHINESE	Stars outlining form	Zodiacal constellation.
EAST INDIAN	White horse with flaming mane	The sun.
RUSSIAN	Natural or conventional form	Emblem of marriage, as human homemaking and happiness.
ROMAN	Natural or conventional form	Emblem of Castor, patron god of horsemen.
SCANDINAVIAN	Natural or conventional form	Emblem of Frey as the sun's speed.
WELSH	Gray horse	Emblem of Satan
	THE DEER	
CHINESE	Conventional form	Symbol of honor and success.
JAPANESE	Conventional form	Emblem of Juro-jin, god of wisdom.
	THE ELEPHANT	
EAST INDIAN	Dark colored	The incarnation of Indra.
	When white	Reincarnation of Buddha.
DANISH	Natural form	Emblem of Denmark, representing a royal traveler to the East.
	THE WOLF	
SCANDINAVIAN	Natural form	Emblem of Odin, the sun god.

Country	Symbol	Signification
	THE WOLF—CONTINUED	
SCANDINAVIAN	Twin wolves	Emblem of Geri and Freki.
ROMAN	Female wolf	Emblem of Remus and Romulus as their foster mother and the nourishing guardian of Rome.
	THE SHEEP	
GRECIAN AND ROMAN	Lamb skin	Emblem of Jason and the Order of the Golden Fleece, signifying the sun.
EGYPTIAN	Ram's head or full form	Emblem of Mendes and of Khnemu.
CHINESE	Stars outlining form of ram	Zodiacal constellation.
HEBREW	Natural form	Zodiacal constellation of Aries.
	THE CAMEL	
EAST INDIAN	Natural form	Patience, long suffering.
PERSIAN	Natural form	Comes home to camp, like poet's cares.
	THE HARE	
CHINESE	The hare in the moon	Signifying untiring industry.
	Stars outlining hare	Constellation.
	THE PIG	
CHINESE	Stars outlining form	Zodiacal constellation.
	THE MONKEY	
CHINESE	Stars outlining form	Zodiacal constellation.
JAPANESE	Natural form	Attributes of Koshin and god of roads. These are Mi-Zaru who sees no evil. Kiki-Zaru who hears no evil. Iwa-Zaru who speaks no evil.

Country	Symbol	Signification
EARLY CHRISTIAN AND MODERN FORM		
THE LION		
IN GENERAL	Natural or conventional form	Christ as the Lion of the tribe of Judah. Strength. Guardianship. Emblem of St. Natalia, St. Germanicus.
IN GENERAL	Lion with wings	Emblem of St. Mark. Cognizance, of Venice.
	Aged lion	Emblem of St. Jerome who took thorn out of foot. Gratitude.
THE TIGER		
IN GENERAL	Natural or conventional form	Bloodthirstiness.
THE WOLF		
IN GENERAL	Natural or conventional form	Rapacity. Rapine. Hunger.
THE FOX		
IN GENERAL	Natural or conventional form	Symbol of craft. Cunning. Intemperance.
THE OX		
IN GENERAL	Natural or conventional form	Emblem of St. Luke, who wrote of the sacrificial nature of Christ.
THE CALF		
IN GENERAL	Natural or conventional form	Emblem of the Prodidigal Son's return. Weakness.
THE HORSE		
IN GENERAL	White horse	Virginity in manhood. The conquering Christian.
	Red horse	Symbol of war.
	Pale gray horse	Dissolution.
THE CAT		
IN GENERAL	Natural or conventional form	Love of freedom. Spite.

Country	Symbol	Signification
THE LAMB		
IN GENERAL	Natural or conventional form	Emblem of Christ as possessing the lamb's meekness and gentleness. Sacrifice.
	Lamb with banner	Emblem of St. Agnes.
THE DEER		
IN GENERAL	Four stags	Matthew, Mark, Luke and John. Emblem of St. Hubert.
	Stag with crucifix between horns	Emblem of St. Eustace as the zealous Christian hunting for converts.
THE GOAT		
IN GENERAL	Natural or conventional form	Dishonor. Materiality.
THE APE		
IN GENERAL	Natural or conventional form	Sin. Malice. Cunning.
THE ASS		
IN GENERAL	Natural or conventional form	Emblem of flight into Egypt of "Holy Family." Entry into Jerusalem. Emblem of St. Anthony. Humbleness.

FISH

The Christian emblem of the fish was adopted by the early followers of Christ as a secret sign. It may be seen cut in the walls of the catacombs and doubtless served as a finger post to the sanctuary within. It was chosen in Cabalistic fashion by using the Greek word for fish which is composed of the initial letters in the following sentence of that language: "Jesus Christ, Son of God, Saviour."

Country	Symbol	Signification
HEBREW AND PAGAN FORM		
EGYPTIAN	The dolphin	Emblem of Isis, wife of the sun god Osiris. Hathor, goddess of beauty. A marriage emblem.
JAPANESE		Reproductiveness.
GRECIAN		Symbol of Aphrodite, goddess of beauty and fecundity. Poseidon, god of the sea. Apollo, god of the sun. The hero Ulysses as a sea traveler.
SCANDINAVIAN		Emblem of Fria, goddess of beauty and fecundity.
	The carp	Emblem of the boy, signifying ambition and success. The Samurai fish because indifferent to physical suffering.
JAPANESE	The red tai	Emblem of Ebisu, god of fish.
ROMAN AND HERALDIC	Cuttle fish	Emblem of Neptune, god of the sea.
	Hippocamp or sea horse	Healing.
	Sea lion	Symbol of boldness.
	Sea dog	Symbol of fidelity.
HEBREW	Twin fishes	The Zodiacal constellation Pisces. Emblem of February.

Country	Symbol	Signification
	FISH—CONTINUED	
HEBREW	Crab	The constellation Cancer. Emblem of summer.
CHINESE	The tortoise	Divination because it carries mystic tablet on back.
JAPANESE	Tortoise with flaming tail	Longevity.

EARLY CHRISTIAN FORM

THE FISH

IN GENERAL	Conventional or natural form	Emblem of Christ. (See heading.) Emblem of Peter as fisher of men. Emblem of Tobias.
	Fish with key in mouth	Emblem of St. Benno.
	Fish with anchor	Hope in Christ.
	The whale	Symbol of Jonah.

BIRDS

"There are two works which bear the title of 'Edda,' the one in verse, the other in prose. The first may be considered a symbolical work of the Scandinavian mythology; the latter a kind of commentary on the first."—*Grenville Pigott.*

Edda means great-grandmother. The folklore of the Elder Edda treats of heroic deeds, superstitions and myths. The Younger Edda is a compilation of fables, metaphors and rhetorical treatises.

Country	Symbol	Signification
	HEBREW AND PAGAN FORM	
	THE EAGLE	
EGYPTIAN	Natural or conventional form	The sun symbol.
ASSYRIAN	Natural or conventional form	Emblem of Nisroch.
ANCIENT HEBREW	Natural or conventional form	The divine spirit.
GRECIAN	With thunderbolt in claw	Vigilance. Majesty.
PHRYGIAN	Double headed	Double vision.
ROMAN	Natural or conventional form	Emblem of Jupiter, chief of the gods. The Roman Legions.
GRECIAN	In connection with Ganymede, the cup bearer of Zeus	Symbol of abduction.
CHINESE	Natural or conventional form	Sovereignty.
JAPANESE	White eagle	Emblem of Jimmu Tenno, the first emperor. Divine right of kings.
	THE PHOENIX	
EGYPTIAN	Bennu, a bird believed to rise from its own ashes	Immortality.

Country	Symbol	Signification
	THE PHOENIX—CONTINUED	
PERSIAN	Semorg, bird with head of a woman	Prosperity. Vehicle of Mahomet.
CHINESE	Feng Wang, which is half peacock and half pheasant	Zodiacal constellation of the South. Appears before a propitious reign. Emblem of summer.
JAPANESE	Ho Ho. Half pheasant and half peacock	Emblem of the Empress.
	THUNDER BIRDS	
PERUVIAN PERSIAN, SABINE	Probably wood peckers	Presage of storm.
RUSSIAN, FINNISH		Guardian of treasures.
	THE STORK	
CHINESE AND JAPANESE	Natural or conventional form	Longevity.
JAPANESE	The cormorant	Emblem of Kushiyatama-no-kami, deity of the eight offerings.
	THE HAWK	
EGYPTIAN	Full form or head	Emblem of Horus, son of Osiris, as keen visioned.
	THE VULTURE	
EGYPTIAN	Full form or head	Emblem of Mut, goddess of the South and the North.
EAST INDIAN	Natural or conventional form	Scavenger of the earth.
	THE GOOSE	
SCANDINAVIAN	Natural or conventional form	Emblem of Freya, the northern Venus.
ROMAN	Natural or conventional form	Emblem of Juno, as it cackles the sunrise for her.
JAPANESE	Wild geese flying	Manhood.

Country	Symbol	Signification
THE COCK		
CHINESE	Stars outlining form	Zodiacal constellation.
	When on a drum	Symbol of peace as drum shows disuse.
	Cock's comb and pheas–ant's plume together	Bravery, prosperity.
JAPANESE	When on torii or gate	Emblem of Amaterasu, as it crows the sunrise for her.
THE DUCK		
JAPANESE	Pair of Mandarin ducks	Conjugal affection as they live and die in pairs.
THE RAVEN		
ASSYRIAN	Natural or conventional form	Messenger of the gods.
SCANDINAVIAN		Emblem of Woden.
ROMAN		Emblem of Apollo.
THE OWL		
EGYPTIAN	Full form or head	Emblem of Amem-Ra
JAPANESE	Natural or conventional form	Filial ingratitude.
WELSH		Emblem of Blodeuwedd, the unfaithful.
GRECIAN		Emblem of Pallas Athena as goddess of wisdom.
THE CUCKOO		
FINNISH	Natural or conventional form	Emblem of Aino. Tears. Desolation.
THE SWAN		
GRECIAN	Natural or conventional form	Emblem of Aphrodite, goddess of beauty.

Country	Symbol	Signification

THE SWAN—CONTINUED

Country	Symbol	Signification
ROMAN		Emblem of Venus, goddess of beauty. Leda, mother of Helen.

THE DOVE

Country	Symbol	Signification
GRECIAN	Natural or conventional form	Emblem of Dodona as prophetic messengers. Emblem of Aphrodite as her aerial steeds.
	Turtle dove	Constancy.

EARLY CHRISTIAN AND MODERN FORM

THE EAGLE

Country	Symbol	Signification
IN GENERAL	Natural or conventional form	Emblem of St. John the Revelator as having perfect vision. Theology. Emblem of U. S. A. as signifying eternal vigilance.
	Double headed	Emblem of Holy Roman Empire, Flanders, Austro-Hungary and Russia.
	Young eagles flying upward	The Ascension.
	Eagle plunging into water to renew youth	Regeneration by baptism.

THE DOVE

Country	Symbol	Signification
IN GENERAL	Single, usually flying	Holy Ghost, or Spirit. Peace.
	Moving over waters	The creation.
	Shedding rays of light	Spiritual blessing.
	Perched on shoulder	Inspiration.
	A pair of turtle doves	Offering at Presentation in the Temple.
	Palm branch in beak	Victory over death.
	On each side of a cup	The Eucharist.
	With serpent's tail	Combination of wisdom and peace.
	With olive branch	Signifying the deluge.

Country	Symbol	Signification
	THE RAVEN	
IN GENERAL	With bread in beak	Emblem of Elijah. St. Benedict.
	Natural or conventional form	Melancholy. Stubbornness.
	THE SWALLOW	
IN GENERAL	Natural form	Emblem of summer.
	THE SPARROW	
IN GENERAL	Natural form	The traveler. Vandalism.
	THE NIGHTINGALE	
IN GENERAL	Natural form	Harmony. Exclusiveness.
	THE THRUSH	
IN GENERAL	Natural form	Melodiousness.
	THE WREN	
IN GENERAL	Natural form	Modesty.
	THE STORK	
IN GENERAL	Natural form	The bearer of the new born.
	THE SWAN	
IN GENERAL	Natural or conventional form	Solitude. Emblem of St. Hubert of Lincoln.
	THE COCK	
IN GENERAL	Natural or conventional form	Emblem of Peter, who denied his Lord.
	THE PARTRIDGE	
IN GENERAL	Natural form	Parental affection.

INSECTS

(Natural and Fictitious)

The scarab is a model in pottery or stone of the sacred beetle of the Egyptians. It has been rightly named "A portable historic document," for the flat side of each scarab is engraved with signs, which, when translated, give the history of the owner. These personal seals were buried with the mummy after decease. As many as three hundred scarabs have been found on one royal mummy. They ceased to be used in 500 B.C.

Country	Symbol	Signification
	HEBREW AND PAGAN FORM	
	The Beetle	
EGYPTIAN	Stone or pottery model known as the scarab, inscribed to	1. Signify mythological deities or events. 2. Names and ranks of historic personages. 3. Names of animals and plants. 4. Funeral signs. 5. Amulets to protect wearers. 6. Signature or official mark. 7. Bearing quotations from the Book of the Dead and placed in the heart cavity of the mummy.
	The Locust	
JUDEAN	Natural form	Scourge. Appetite.
	The Bat	
CHINESE	Natural or conventional form	Contentment. Happiness.
	Five bats	Wealth, longevity, health, love of virtue, peaceful end.
	The Scorpion	
HEBREW	Stars outlining form	Zodiacal constellation. Emblem of October.
	The Chameleon	
IN GENERAL	Natural form	Changeableness.

Country	Symbol	Signification
EARLY CHRISTIAN AND MODERN FORM		
THE BEE		
IN GENERAL	Natural or conventional form	Industry. Diligence. Emblem of Napoleon and Beethoven.
THE ANT		
IN GENERAL	Natural form	Community spirit.
THE FLY		
IN GENERAL	Natural form	Pestilence.
THE GNAT		
IN GENERAL	Natural form	Torment. Irritation.
THE SPIDER		
IN GENERAL	When weaving	Patience. Subtility. Emblem of Arachné.
THE SNAIL		
IN GENERAL	Natural form	Fruitfulness.
FIREFLIES		
JAPANESE	Natural form	Ghosts of slain warriors.

THE SERPENT

"Symbolism was the essence of the genius of the Egyptian nation."—*Lenormant.*

Ophites—A Gnostic sect who believed that the serpent in the Garden of Eden was the impersonation of Divine Wisdom and the Teacher of Men.

Country	Symbol	Signification
HEBREW AND PAGAN FORM		
THE COBRA		
EGYPTIAN	With head erect, ringed skin and swelling throat	Sovereignty. Generative power of the sun.
EAST INDIAN	Seven headed	Emblem of Naga.
THE ASP		
EGYPTIAN	Head erect, short thick body	Royalty. Divine goodness and immortality.
THE COLUBER		
EGYPTIAN	Long body and head in horizontal position.	Destroyer of souls.
THE SERPENT		
CHINESE	Stars outlining form	Zodiacal constellation. Fertility.
GRECIAN AND ROMAN	Twin serpents, coiled about a wand, with heads erect	Emblem of Aesculapius founder of medicine. Symbol of Hermes and Mercury.
GRECIAN AND ROMAN	Twined as curls about a face with staring eyes	Emblem of the Gorgon Medusa, whose hair was changed to serpents.
GRECIAN	Coiled on shield of Athena or at her feet	Emblem of her foster son, Erecthonios, whom as a child she kept in a chest with the serpent of wisdom.
POMPEIAN	Natural or conventional form	Household gods (Lares and Penates), gods of fertility.

Country	Symbol	Significacation
THE SERPENT—CONTINUED		
MEXICAN	Feathered serpent	Emblem of Quetzalcoatl, Aztec, "Fair god." Patron of law-order and agriculture.
SCANDINAVIAN	Serpent with tail in its mouth, forming a circle (Jörmungund).	The Universe.
JUDEAN	Brazen serpent of Moses' time	Healing.
THE ADDER		
JUDEAN	With one ear to the ground and stopping other ear with her tail	Prudence.
THE SALAMANDER		
FRENCH	Allied to the lizard and frog	Emblem of Francis the first. Immune to fire.
THE BASILISK		
HERALDIC	Crested head, erect and piercing eyes	Cruelty. Mesmerism.

EARLY CHRISTIAN AND MODERN FORM

THE SERPENT

Country	Symbol	Significacation
IN GENERAL	Natural or conventional form	Evil overcome by good.
	Crawling on ground	Sin. Subtility.
	With Adam and Eve	Knowledge of good and evil.
ELIZABETHAN	Head erect	Human wisdom.
OPHITES	Natural form	Emblem of Christ as perfect wisdom.
THE CROCODILE		
IN GENERAL	Natural form	Dissimulation.

FABULOUS CREATURES

"With savages, most religions sprang from a desire to propitiate by worship those powers from whom they feared that some injury may be done."—*Fergusson.*

Among the descendants of Shem, son of Noah, were the Assyrians, Phoenicians, Arabians and Hebrews, but the latter were the only people among those tribes who believed in one God and no lesser deities. Therefore their ritual was less incumbered by fabulous creatures than any of the others.

Country	Symbol	Signification
HEBREW AND PAGAN FORM		
THE DRAGON		
CHINESE AND JAPANESE	Serpent's body, bulging eyes, horned head and five claws, in clouds and generally pursuing the ball of wisdom	Imperial guardian of the air. Bearer of the imperial dead to Paradise.
	In water or rising above streams, with above form	Imperial guardian of the waters.
	Threading swamps or near fields	Imperial guardian of the marshes.
	When showing only three claws	Dragon of the common people, representing increasing prosperity.
CHINESE	Stars outlining form	Zodiacal constellation of the East.
JAPANESE	Chinese form with eyes gazing upward	Spiritual guardian of the faith.
	The same with eyes gazing downward	Earthly guardian of the faith.
EAST INDIAN	Usual form	Guardian of the faith.
ROMAN	Dragon chained to a rock	Symbol of Perseus and Andromeda.
HERALDIC	Hydra or seven headed dragon	Terror. Destruction.
	Winged dragons facing arms	Guardianship.

Country	Symbol	Signification
	THE SPHINX	
EGYPTIAN	Body of lion and human head	Strength and intelligence.
	Body of lion with hawk's head	Emblem of Horus as guardian of the body of Osiris.
	Body of lion with ram's head	Emblem of Khnemu, the maker of stars.
GRECIAN	Body of lion, breast and head of a woman	Pestilence. Secrecy.
PERSIAN	Andro-Sphinx Bird's body, man's legs and scorpion's tail	Emblem of the Magian Genius of Prophecy.
	THE CENTAUR	
GRECIAN	A horse's body with a man's shoulders, arms and head	Brute force.
HEBREW	A horse's body with a man's shoulders, arms and head	Zodiacal constellation known as Sagittarius, the archer.
	THE HARPY	
GRECIAN	Head and breast of a woman, body of a vulture	Torment. Voracious appetite.
	THE SIREN	
IN GENERAL	Half woman, half fish	Allurement. Entanglement. Dangerous affection.
ROMAN	Circe, who changed captives into beasts	Baleful attraction. Sorcery.
	THE GRIFFIN	
GRECIAN	Lion's body, eagle or vulture head	Emblem of Alexander the Great.
IN GENERAL	Lion's body, eagle or vulture head	Invincibility.

Country	Symbol	Signification
	THE UNICORN	
CHINESE	Chilin. Body of antelope with single horn	Prosperity. Peace.
JAPANESE	The Kirin. Body of deer with single horn	Virtue. Radiant beauty.
MOHAMMEDAN	Body of antelope with single horn	Chastity.

EARLY CHRISTIAN AND MODERN FORM

	THE DRAGON	
IN GENERAL	Resembling Chinese form and depicted under foot	Emblem of St. Michael. St. George. Evil crushed to earth.
	When chained	Emblem of St. John of Rheims.
	With a staff	Emblem of St. Margaret.
	When winged	Emblem of St. Sylvester.
IN GENERAL	"The great red dragon"	Lust.
	THE UNICORN	
IN GENERAL AND HERALDIC	Body of a horse, tail of a lion, hoofs of a stag, central long horn, protruding outward	Chastity.

ANGELIC PERSONAGES

"Knowledge of Christian symbolism is requisite for those who study ancient illuminations, sculptures, stained glass and other decorative arts. It is absolutely necessary for the architect and student of mediaeval architecture to have a thorough acquaintance with the art which guided its early masters."—*W. and G. Audsley.*

Country	Symbol	Signification
	HEBREW AND PAGAN FORM	
	ANGELS	
JUDEAN	Michael, Gabriel, Suriel, Raphael, Tauthaboth, Eratooth.	Celestial service.
EGYPTIAN AND ASSYRIAN	The good Genii	Celestial service. Bearers of water for the Tree of Life.
EAST INDIAN	The Vedic Apsaris.	Charmers of the blest.
BUDDHISTIC	As Bodhisatvas and Rakan	Sanctified service of saints, once mortals.
MOHAMMEDAN	Houri, dark-eyed maidens; beings which have never been mortals	In the service of the blest.
	ARCHANGELS	
	Michael	
	Gabriel	Conductor.
	Asrafil	Recording Angel.
	Israfel	Herald of the Resurrection.
SCANDINAVIAN	Valkyria	Ministering angels of Valhalla or Hall of the Blest. Attendants of Odin.
	The Nornies	Bearers of sacred water to Yggdrasil.
CHINESE	The seven worthies	Knowledge of happiness.
	The Genii who live upon air and ride to heaven on the back of a dragon	Rulers of spirits.

Country	Symbol	Signification
	EARLY CHRISTIAN FORM	
	THE NINE CHOIRS WHICH ARE	
IN GENERAL	1. Archangels	Celestial ministry.
	2. Angels	
	3. Cherubim	
	4. Seraphim	
	5. Thrones	
	6. Dominions	
	7. Virtues	
	8. Powers	
	9. Principalities	
	THE ARCHANGELS—PRIMARY	
	1. Michael, Captain of the host	Divine likeness.
	2. Gabriel, annunciation and resurrection	Divine power.
	3. Uriel, leader of Seraphim	Divine light.
	4. Raphael	Divine restorer.
	SECONDARY	
	5. Zophiel	Leaders of choirs.
	6. Zadkiel	
	7. Hamiel	
	8. Camiel	
	9. Zaphkiel	
	The Seraphim are represented by infants' heads, surrounded by six wings: the two upper and two lower are crossed	Guardians of the Throne.
	The Cherubim are represented by infants' heads between two wings	Signify adoration and protection.

Country		Symbol	Signification
		EARLY CHRISTIAN FORM ANGELS—CONTINUED	
IN GENERAL		Angels bearing sceptres	The Dominion of God.
		Angels bearing musical instruments	Felicity in Heaven.
		Angels bearing trumpets	The voice of Deity.
		Angels with censers	Prayers.
		Angels with garments belted	In the active service of Deity.
		Angels without sandals	Heavenly service only.
		Cloud or circle of angels	Spiritual ecstasy.
		Angels	Loving thoughts.

THE HALO AND THE CROWN

"Mithraic (early Persian) bas-reliefs cut on the faces of rocks, or on stone tablets, abound in the countries formerly the Western Provinces of the Holy Roman Empire, exist in Germany, still more in France and in England, on the line of the Picts (early tribe) wall and the noted ones at Bath. Insomuch as Bel, the Semitic sun god, was the great divinity of the Druids, it is easy to see what a ready acceptance the worship of his more refined Persian equivalent (Mithra) would find among Celtic races when once introduced by the Roman troops and colonists, many of whom were Orientals."—*C. W. King, M.A.*

Country	Symbol	Signification
HEBREW AND PAGAN FORM		
THE HALO		
EAST INDIAN, JAPANESE AND CHINESE	Circular or trefoil, whether plain or decorated	The triad god. The sun's rays. Sanctity.
JUDEAN	Two rayed halo of Moses, appearing also as horns	Truth and Justice.
THE CROWN		
EGYPTIAN	When composed of solar disk and two falcon feathers	Emblem of Theban, sun god. Amem-Ra.
	Disk with goat horns	Emblem of Isis, signifying life and strength.
	White crown shaped like a cone	Crown of upper Egypt.
	Red crown shaped like a band with a peak	Crown of lower Egypt, generally worn by Neith, as goddess of hunting and weaving.
	Red and white crown, together; one within the other	Double crown of Egypt, generally worn by Mut, the Theban divine mother, as well as other chief gods.
	Shuti crown of ten double ostrich plumes	Signifies power to divide the heavens and enter therein.

Country	Symbol	Signification

THE CROWN—CONTINUED

Country	Symbol	Signification
EGYPTIAN	Atef crown composed of asps, horns and plumes, circling the white crown of upper Egypt	Generally worn by Thoth as master of law.

THE WREATH

Country	Symbol	Signification
GRECIAN AND ROMAN	When of cypress leaves	Symbol of Pluto, Chief of Hades.
	When of oak leaves	Symbol of Zeus or Jupiter, as the father god.
	When of pine leaves	Symbol of Pan as Nature's king.
	When of laurel leaves	Symbol of Apollo and the Muse Clio.
	When of willow leaves	Symbol of Hera as a part of her residence tree.
	When of myrtle leaves	Symbol of the bride.

EARLY CHRISTIAN AND MODERN FORM

THE HALO

Country	Symbol	Signification
IN GENERAL	Known as the Nimbus when circling the head only	
	As Aureola, when circling head and shoulders	Sanctification.
	Known as the Glory, when circling entire figure	

THE NIMBUS

Country	Symbol	Signification
IN GENERAL	When circular and plain or with three rays or with the Greek letters O Ω N—I Am	Emblem of the First Person of the Trinity.
	When bearing Greek cross or Lamb or rays	Second Person of the Trinity.

Country	Symbol	Signification
THE NIMBUS-CONTINUED		
IN GENERAL	When square	Symbol of distinction only.
THE CROWN		
IN GENERAL	Usual form	Symbol of the Virgin Mary.
	When at feet of Saints	Signifying noble birth.
	When worn on the head	Emblem of royal birth.
	When held in the right hand	Symbol of the Virtues.
	When of thorns	Emblem of the crucifixion. The Delphic Sibyl, who prophesied the suffering of the Saviour.
THE CORONA		
IN GENERAL	Crown of lights used in churches on special occasions	The Resurrection.
THE GARLAND OR CHAPLET		
IN GENERAL	As a circlet	The crown of beauty. Wreath of poetry.
	When used as a continuous motif in decoration	Exuberance of life. Joy. Mirth.
THE MITRE		
IN GENERAL	The two points of a bishop's crown or mitre, which is usually of cloth studded with gems	The Old and New Testaments.
DUCAL CROWN		
ENGLISH	Designed in strawberry leaves	Companionship with royalty.

THE CROSS AND THE MONOGRAM

"By these outward forms early Christians were inspired with feelings of devotion and love and in the absence of books derived from them their chief knowledge of objects made sacred by usage. To the unlearned they spoke a clear and intelligible language; that they were full of poetry, no one who will endeavor to interpret them can doubt."—*Louisa Twining.*

"The cross, the priestly robes and symbols are all anterior to the Christian era by thousands of years."—*Alexander Wilder, M.D.*

Country	Symbol	Signification
	HEBREW AND PAGAN FORM	
	THE CROSS	
HINDU	The Swastica or fylfot cross	"It is." The sacred fire of Heaven.

BUDDHISTIC		Emblem of Gautama Buddha as the Enlightened One.
NORTH AMERICAN INDIAN		The four winds of Heaven. Prosperity.

THE TAU CROSS IN FORM OF CAPITAL T

BABYLONIAN		Emblem of Thamumez, sun god, consort of Ashtoreth.
EGYPTIAN		Signifies to live. Hidden wisdom. Emblem of early Egypt.

Country	Symbol	Signification

THE CROSS—CONTINUED

Country	Symbol	Signification
ROMAN		Sign of omission (as when placed upon houses where child was to be spared during the Massacre of the Innocents.)
		Emblem of Hellespontine Sibyl.

CRUX ANSATA OR KEY OF LIFE ANKH

EGYPTIAN	The tau surmounted by circle of eternity in elliptical form	Immortality. Eternal life.

EARLY CHRISTIAN AND MODERN FORM

IN GENERAL	The original or tree cross	"The accursed tree." Humiliation.

THE CROSS

IN GENERAL	With equal arms	Christianity. The Greek cross.

	Greek cross of red color	Symbol of the Rosicrucians. The Templars. Red Cross Society.

Country	Symbol	Signification
	THE CROSS—CONTINUED	
IN GENERAL	With vertical arm extended above horizontal arm	The Crucifixion. The Latin cross.
	With double horizontal arms	Emblem of an archbishop.
	With triple horizontal arms	Emblem of the Pope.
	In form of letter X	Martyrdom. The saltire or St. Andrew's cross (as this saint was martyred on this form.)
ENGLISH	Composed of four hammer-like crosses	Known as the Canterbury cross.

Country	Symbol	Signification
	THE CROSS—CONTINUED	
RUSSIAN	The Latin cross with one half of St. Andrew's cross strapped across lower portion of upright arm	Emblem of Christ and St. Andrew, the first Christian missionary to Russia. The Slavonic cross.

| IN GENERAL | Of equal arms shaped like fishes' tails | Emblem of Freemasons. The eight Beatitudes. The Maltese cross. |

| | The Latin cross with vertical arm pointed at base in order to fix in the ground | Signifying the Soldiers of the Cross. The Crusaders' cross. |
| | Either Greek or Latin cross with three balls at end of arms | Heraldic cross called Batonné. |

Country	Symbol	Signification
	THE CROSS—CONTINUED	
IN GENERAL	Either Greek or Latin form with one ball or apple at the ends	Heraldic device called Pommé.
	Composed of four tau crosses	Heraldic device called cross potent.
	Composed of cross potent and Greek cross	Known as the Jerusalem cross.
	Either Greek or Latin form with three leaves at point	Heraldic device called cross Fleuré.
CELTIC	Latin cross with circle of eternity	Immortality.

Country	Symbol	Signification
	THE CROSS—CONTINUED	
IN GENERAL	Latin cross worn on the breast	The Pectoral cross.
	Latin cross placed at wayside or well	Pilgrims' prayers.
	Latin cross made with receptacle in centre to hold sacred bread	The Monstrance, signifying the Eucharist or Communion.
	Latin cross with receptacle to hold relics of saints	The Reliquary, Sacred Memories.
	Latin cross affixed to a loft or beam or screen	The Roodcross. Faith.
ENGLISH	Public crosses	The heart of the town.
	Roadside crosses	Right of sanctuary.
	Boundary crosses	Limited rights.
	Memorial crosses	Sacred ground.
	Preaching crosses	Age of faith.
	Grave crosses	Immortality through Christ.
	The processional cross when borne before a bishop	Jurisdiction.

Country	Symbol	Signification

Two Monograms

Country	Symbol	Signification
IN GENERAL	The letter P combined with letter X or the first two letters of the Greek word for Christ	Monogram of the Saviour. The cross of Constantine or the portentious sign which he saw in the heavens. The precious sign or portent.

| | I. H. S. Initials of sentence "Jesus Homenum Salvator" (Jesus Saviour of men) | Monogram of the Saviour. The Precious Emblem. |

DEMONS, SATYRS AND NYMPHS

"A lover of the Bible is a philosopher of the highest class: for that word by its derivation signifies a lover of wisdom, from the Greek word 'philos,' lover, and 'sophia,' wisdom. From these premises it is clear that a desire to relegate to the limbo of untaught 'questions' any branch of the religious study, finds no support from the Scriptures. The word devil occurs more than fifty times in the New Testament. The Cinghalese religion consists almost entirely of devil worship. In Ceylon, the fear of the devil is allowed full scope. In Christendom, the fear certainly exists and perhaps a certain degree of reverence, but the form of worship is lacking. This implies indirect or negative worship."—*E. Turney.*

Country	Symbol	Signification
HEBREW AND PAGAN FORM		
DEMONS		
EGYPTIAN	Typhon, sometimes as a serpent or sometimes as the Nile	Destruction.
PERSIAN	The bad genii	Evil influence.
	Ahriman	The spirit of evil.
ASSYRIAN	Gibil the evil one	Destruction.
	The fire fiend	Devastation.
ARABIAN	The Jinns or fiends	Sorcery.
	The devil bird	Presage of evil.
GRECIAN	Hecate or female devil	Sorceress of the infernal regions.
	Medusa, the woman with snake curls	Annihilation.
	Cyclops or one eyed gigantic devils	Demoniacal strength.
ROMAN	Pluto	Chief of the infernal regions.
	The devil fish or octopus	Malignancy.
SCANDINAVIAN	Meming	Demoniacal forger of weapons.

Country	Symbol	Signification
DEMONS—CONTINUED		
SCANDINAVIAN	Erictho	Sorcery in the forest.
	The Galdrankinna	Interference with affairs of the heart.
CHINESE	With man's form though abnormal	Evil influence.
JAPANESE	Emma o, chief of ten devils in Hades	Regent of Hades and demoniacal scribe.
	Oni or attendant devils, such as bewitched foxes and badgers	False leaders.
	The Tengu, long nosed goblins	Demoniacal swordsmanship.
ORKNEY ISLANDS	The Skow or devil	Kidnapper of church goers.
ENGLISH AND IRISH	Will-o-the-Wisp Jack-o-Lantern	False lights that lure the unwary.
	The Banshee	Messenger of fatalities.
	The Elves (evil)	Sylvan mischief makers.
GERMAN	Wicked elves and Gnomes	Glee in mischief.
SCOTTISH	Haxa, the druidess	The Sorceress.
SATYRS AND FAUNS		
GRECIAN	Man's body, goat's horns, tail and hoofs	Lasciviousness. Revelry.
SCOTTISH	Ourisk or the Highland satyr	Freebooting.
NYMPHS		
GREEK AND ROMAN	Feminine wood creatures, consorts of satyrs	License; lawlessness; the light-footed; beautiful but soulless.

Country	Symbol	Signification

EARLY CHRISTIAN AND MODERN FORM

DEMONS

Country	Symbol	Signification
IN GENERAL	Mephistopheles Prince of Darkness Lucifer Satan Adversary The Wicked One Beelzebub	Ferocity, Sorcery, Lust, Lunacy, Tyranny, Egotism, Rebellion, Deceit.
	A devil. Judas Iscariot (John 6:70)	Disloyalty.
	The Possessed (Luke 9:39)	Necromancy.
	The son of the devil (John 8:44)	Heritage.
	The demon cup as defined (1 Cor. 10:21)	The cup of sorcery.

WITCHES

Country	Symbol	Signification
IN GENERAL	The witch of Endor	Phantasy. Foresight for evil.

GEOMETRICAL FORMS

"Every ornament to deserve the name, must possess an appropriate meaning and be introduced with an intelligent purpose. The symbolic association of each ornament must be understood; otherwise things beautiful in themselves will be rendered absurd by their application."—*A. W. Pugin.*

Country	Symbol	Signification
	HEBREW AND PAGAN FORM	
	THE CIRCLE	
EGYPTIAN	When representing the sun or moon	Eternity.
	When placed on a dish	Sacred bread used as altar offerings.
ASSYRIAN	When winged and enclosing figure of Assur, the sun god	Immortality.
EAST INDIAN	Three circles joined together	Signify Brahma the Creator, Vishnu the preserver and Siva the destroyer.
SCANDINAVIAN	Circle with one dot in the center	Emblem of Freya, goddess of beauty.
	With three dots in the center	Symbol of the triad god.
EGYPTIAN	As solid circle or globe with wings of aspi-ration, horns of strength and serpents of wisdom	Emblem of Osiris, the sun god and judge of the Dead. Antidote to evil.
ROMAN	Full form or crescent	Emblem of Diana, goddess of hunting.
MOHAMMEDAN	Crescent and star	Emblem of the faith. National arms of Turkish Empire.
	THE WHEEL	
EGYPTIAN	Natural or conventional form	The sun.

Country	Symbol	Signification
	THE WHEEL—CONTINUED	
BUDDHISTIC	The Chakra	Wheel of law and prayer.
	THE SQUARE	
CHINESE AND JAPANESE	Usual form	The earth.
	When placed within a circle	Heaven and earth.
CHALDEAN AND JUDEAN	Usual form	The perfect form or plan.
ROMAN	When referring to the Roman Quadrata or ancient symbol stone	Emblem of ancient city which was built square.
MOHAMMEDAN	When referring to the Caaba or sacred square stone and temple of the Prophet at Mecca.	Emblem of the faith.
	LINE	
CHINESE AND JAPANESE	When vertical	Signifies the masculine in nature.
	When horizontal or curved	Signifies the feminine in nature
EGYPTIAN	Zig zag	Water. The Nile river.
NORMAN	Zig zag	Life's course.
HERALDIC	When invected or ingrailed (scalloped)	Land.
EGYPTIAN, GRECIAN AND ROMAN	Meandering lines such as the Doric fret, etc.	Continuity of life.
CHINESE AND JAPANESE	When used as a chain Ogee or double curved line	Continuity of life. Balance and support.
IN GENERAL	When in the form of a labyrinth	Emblem of ancient mystical grove or woodland. Sacrificial temple.

Country	Symbol	Signification
THE TRIANGLE		
EGYPTIAN	When used as emblem of Osiris, Isis and Horus	Signifies intelligence, matter and cosmos.
SCANDINAVIAN	Usual form	Emblem of the triad god.
EAST INDIAN	When pointing upward	Emblem of Siva as god of fire.
	When pointing downward	Emblem of Vishnu as god of water.
	Both forms intersecting	Creation of fire and water.
JUDEAN	With unequal sides and two Hebrew letters of Jehovah's name	The Almighty.
	Double and intersecting	The seal of Solomon. The positive and negative attributes of creation.
THE RECTANGLE		
EGYPTIAN, GRECIAN AND MEXICAN	When used as base for tombs and altars	Sacred form of the faith.
THE PENTAGON		
IN GENERAL	When used as a pentagram or five sided object and the pentacle or five pointed star	Divination.
THE HEPTAGON		
EAST INDIAN	A figure of seven sides and seven angles, as—	Brahma's palace or the divine abode.
THE OCTAGON		
CHINESE	A figure of eight sides and eight angles, containing the eight trigrams or mystical lines introduced by an ancient sage, and the design known as the Pakwa	The path of life.

Country	Symbol	Signification
	THE OCTAGON—CONTINUED	
JAPANESE	Usual form	Emblem of heaven's palace of eight sides. Residence of goddess on Fuji mountain.

EARLY CHRISTIAN AND MODERN FORM

THE CIRCLE

Country	Symbol	Signification
IN GENERAL	Usual form	Eternity. Masonic boundary line of duty.
	When above head	Sanctity.
	In crescent form when beneath feet of Virgin	Dominion.

THE SQUARE

Country	Symbol	Signification
IN GENERAL	A figure of four sides and four angles	The Christian. The New Jerusalem. Honesty.
	When placed within a circle	Eternity of life.

KNOTS AND ENLACEMENTS (WHEN ENDLESS)

Country	Symbol	Signification
EARLY CELTS	Runic knot	Love of God.
JUDEAN	Solomon's knot	Wisdom.
	True lover's knot	Fidelity.
ITALIAN	Enlacement in any form	Emblem of the Comancine builders. The joy of Christian living.

THE HEXAGON

Country	Symbol	Signification
IN GENERAL	A figure with six sides and six angles	The attributes of the Creator.

THE HEPTAGON

Country	Symbol	Signification
IN GENERAL	A figure of seven sides and seven angles	The seven churches. Seven angels. Seven lamps. Seven seals.

THE OCTAGON

Country	Symbol	Signification
IN GENERAL	A figure of eight sides and eight angles	Baptism. Regeneration. (Creation in seven days, the eighth represents recreation.)

Country	Symbol	Signification
THE DECAGON		
IN GENERAL	A figure of ten sides and ten angles	Signifying the Disciples, omitting Peter and Judas, the one who denied and the one who betrayed.
THE DODECAGON		
IN GENERAL	A figure of twelve sides and twelve angles	Signifying the twelve Disciples.
THE WHEEL		
IN GENERAL	When winged and of fire and with eyes in wings	Symbol of the thrones or one of the choirs of angels.

ARCHITECTURAL FORMS

History informs us that one of the ancient symbols of the Universe was a cave. The Zoroastrian sect in Persia were among the people who painted upon these caves emblems of nature's forces.

The Ammonites were worshipers of Jupiter in Libya.

Country	Symbol	Signification
HEBREW AND PAGAN FORM		
THE MENHIR AND DOLMEN		
DRUIDICAL	Upright stones raised as altars	Sun altars.
JUDEAN		Emblem of Jacob who raised altar stone to the one God. The Beth-el.
THE COLUMN OR PILLAR		
EGYPTIAN	Column with lotus or papyrus capital	Emblem of the faith.
	When signifying pillars of heaven	Emblem of Nut, Neith, the sky goddess, as representing her arms and limbs.
GRECIAN	The Doric column. A column with plain cushion covered by an abacus or square tablet for its capital	Signifies primitive force.
	The Ionic column. A column with four volutes for its capital	Signifying the influence of education upon primitive force.
	The Corinthian column. A column with acanthus leaves and volutes for its capital	Signifying the beginning of degeneracy in primitive force.
IN GENERAL	A column used singly as a monument in any style	Distinction. Dominion.

Country	Symbol	Signification
THE COLUMN OR PILLAR—CONTINUED		
VENETIAN	When used as a gondola hitching post and decorated with coat of arms belonging to family owning the post	Emblem of distinction.
	When striped with red and white	Emblem of the barber, who, in ancient times was a surgeon and used this sign of a bandaged limb.
THE GATE		
EGYPTIAN	The Pylon	Entrance to the sanctuary. Barriers to evil.
JAPANESE	Torii or perch for the fowl which announced the sunrise	Emblem of Amaterasu the sun goddess. Emblem of Inari, the goddess of rice.
IN GENERAL	In various forms	Protection. Safety. Commerce, Judicial assembly.
THE ARCH		
PERSIAN AND PICTISH	In temples or on tomb sculptures	The arch of the sun.
ROMAN	Used singly as a monument	Victory. Dominion.
	Employed in buildings	Hospitality.
THE PAVEMENT		
JUDEAN	The palace floor of Solomon	Emblem of the sea.
ROMAN AND VENETIAN	Mosaic floors in churches and palaces	The movement and color of the sea.
THE DOME AND CENTRE		
IN GENERAL	The dome	The canopy of heaven.
EARLY PERSIAN	The Omphalos or navel. (The origin of the dome.)	The centre of the earth. Symbol of Iran.
EAST INDIAN	Vedic omphalos	Signifying Yama, dwelling on the centre of the earth.

Country	Symbol	Signification
	THE DOME AND CENTRE—CONTINUED	
GRECIAN AND ARABIAN	Centre of dwelling or hearth	Stability.
CHINESE	Centre or apex, the single stone of the stepped temple	Emblem of Shung-ti, the chief of all the gods.
MOKI INDIAN	The Bowl. (Architectural form.)	Emblem of the dome of heaven.
	ROOF AND CEILING	
IN GENERAL	Usual form of roof	Canopy of heaven. Protection. Safety. Hospitality.
EGYPTIAN	Decoration of ceilings. When representing figure of goddess Nut or the sky bending over the earth god Seb and supported by the air god Shu	The elements.
	STEPS OR STAIRS	
CHALDEAN, CHINESE, JAPANESE AND MEXICAN	When erected singly or in groups	Signifying rising stages of mankind toward heaven or highest place.
	THE WALL	
IN GENERAL	Single or double	Barrier. Safety. Prosperity. Distinction.
	THE BRIDGE	
CHINESE AND JAPANESE	In any form	The way of the gods.
	When bowed	Bridge of heaven or rainbow.
MOHAMMEDAN	When of a hair's breadth	Bridge of Paradise which only the righteous are able to cross.

Country	Symbol	Signification
	THE TOWER	
EGYPTIAN	Tat or measuring tower of the Nile. Nilometer.	The steps to heaven.
FEUDAL EUROPEAN	Tall, slender and generally windowless at base	Protection of the church treasures. Watching.
	THE PYRAMID	
EGYPTIAN	Monumental burial places of kings	Fire of the gods. Residence of the dead.

EARLY CHRISTIAN AND MODERN FORM

Country	Symbol	Signification
	THE COLUMN	
IN GENERAL	Usual form	Aspiration of the Christian. The morally strong. The Straightforward.
	THE ARCH	
IN GENERAL	Usual form	The beneficence of God. The hospitality of Christian faith.
	THE DOME	
IN GENERAL	Usual form	Love of God.
RUSSIAN	Cluster of five domes	Signifying the Metropolitan and his four bishops.
	THE DOOR	
ENGLISH	The Western Door of Church	Emblem of Christ.
IN GENERAL	When open	Emblem of welcome. Generosity.
	THE GATE	
IN GENERAL	When golden or pearly	Signifies entrance to heaven.
	When of brass	Signifies entrance to Hades.
	THE TOWER OR STEEPLE	
IN GENERAL	Usual form	Purity. Aspiration. Emblem of St. Barbara who was called the "Ivory tower of purity."

Country	Symbol	Signification
	STEPS OR STAIRS	
IN GENERAL	Usual form	Pilgrimage. Pathway of the seeker after spiritual knowledge.
	GARGOYLES	
IN GENERAL	When represented by grotesque forms	Evil spirits kept on the outside of the church. Scare devils to ward off evil spirits.
	DIVISIONS (EARLY CHRISTIAN CHURCHES)	
IN GENERAL	The bema or centre	The Holy of Holies or Heaven. Sanctity.
	The chorus or approach to the centre	Holy place or probation.
	The narthex or porch to the temple to commemorate porch of Solomon's temple	Penitence. Approach.

MILITARY EMBLEMS

"The decorative beauty of heraldry, far from being that of form and color alone was always an imaginative one depending much on the symbolic meaning of its designs."—*G. W. Eve.*

Country	Symbol	Signification
HEBREW AND PAGAN FORM		
THE SPEAR OR LANCE		
EGYPTIAN	Usual form	Weapon of the king.
CHINESE		Emblem of Kwanyu, god of war.
JAPANESE		Emblem of Isanagi, mythical creator of Japanese. Emblem of Hachiman, god of war.
THE JAVELIN		
JUDEAN	Usual form	Emblem of kingly force. Martial readiness.
THE ARROW		
EGYPTIAN	Two crossed arrows	Symbol of Neith as goddess of the chase.
THE AX		
SCANDINAVIAN	Usual form	Primitive warfare. Emblem of the Vikings.
THE SWORD		
EGYPTIAN	Usual form	The founding of the weapon.
JAPANESE		Emblem of Susano-o, the violent god.
		Symbol of "The soul of the Samurai."
	When double edged	Praying for rain sword.
ARMOUR		
IN GENERAL		Self defense.
	Head piece or helmet when crested	The victor.

Country	Symbol	Signification

THE WINGED HELMET

ROMAN, SCANDINAVIAN		The messenger.

EARLY CHRISTIAN AND MODERN FORM
THE SWORD

IN GENERAL	Flaming sword	Divine wrath. Emblem of Zophiel. Angel of the garden of Eden.
	Usual form	Symbol of St. Paul as the Christian soldier.
	When piercing hand	Emblem of St. Thomas of Canterbury.
	When at feet of saint	Emblem of St. Pantalon.
	When showing acute point	Signifies justice.
	When obtuse point	Signifies religion.
	When blunted point	Signifies mercy.
	When held upright	Consecration. Allegiance.

SPEAR OR LANCE

IN GENERAL	Usual or conventional form	Symbol of St. Michael, St. George, St. Phillip. European Sibyl who prophesied the flight into Egypt.

THE ARROW

IN GENERAL	Usual form	Emblem of St. Sebastian who was martyred by arrows. Emblem of the hunter and of Cupid.

THE DAGGER

IN GENERAL	Misere-corde or small dagger used by ancient monks	Protection against the foe.

THE SLING

IN GENERAL	Pocket with string for holding and slinging stones	Emblem of David who became the king.

Country	Symbol	Signification
	THE BANNER	
IN GENERAL	Usual form	The Christian's victory over the flesh. Triumph. Place. Title. Lineage.
	ARMOUR	
IN GENERAL	"The whole armour"	Protection of God.
	The Spurs	Emblem of Knighthood.
	The Helmet	Signifies courage.
	THE SHIELD	
HERALDIC, ENGLISH	1. When exhibiting chevron or band shaped like a gable	Protection.
	2. The chief or straight band passing across upper third of shield	Guardianship.
	3. The fess or band crossing centre of shield horizontally	Patriotism.
	4. The pale or band crossing shield in centre vertically	Valor.
	5. The bend or band crossing shield diagonally	Knightly service.
	6. The pile, sharp pointed, wedge shaped band crossing shield vertically	Tenacity.
	7. The bend sinister or band crossing from left-hand upper corner of shield to right-hand lower corner	Royal descent.

GEMS

"If I say 'white' or 'purple' in any ordinary line of poetry, they evoke emotions so exclusively that I cannot say why they move me, but if I say them in the same mood, in the same breath with such obviously intellectual symbols as a cross or a crown of thorns, I think of purity and sovereignty." — *W. B. Yeats.*

Country	Symbol	Signification
	HEBREW AND PAGAN FORM	
	THE SARD	
EGYPTIAN	One layer of the onyx, usually red	Blood of Isis. Stone of August.
	JADE	
CHINESE	A hard soapy, sometimes fibrous stone formed by the drippings from mountain lakes in Turkestan which are usually salt water. Near rivers in Burmah	Emblem of the Emperor. Virtue.
	THE HELIOTROPE (SEE BLOODSTONE)	
BABYLONIAN	Usual form	Divination. Sacred stone of the gods. Invulnerability.
	THE JASPER	
EARLY PERSIAN	Crypto-crystalline quartz	Stone of Mithra, god of truth. Stone of friendship.
	THE SAPPHIRE	
EARLY PERSIAN	Blue corundum	The sacred stone.
GRECIAN		Stone of Apollo and September.
EAST INDIAN		Light of the gods. Prosperity.

Country	Symbol	Signification
	GEMS OF AARON'S BREAST PLATE	
JUDEAN	1. Sardius, Topaz, Carbuncle 2. Emerald, Sapphire, Diamond 3. Ligure, Agate, Amethyst 4. Beryl, Onyx, Jasper 5. The Urim and Thummim or jewels of light and perfection. (species unknown)	Divination.
	THE ABRAXUS GEMS	
GNOSTIC	Sard, Jasper, Amethyst	Sacred gems of the divine creator known as "Abraxus," a fabulous creature with a man's body, a lion or cock's head and serpents for legs.

EARLY CHRISTIAN AND MODERN FORM

THE DIAMOND

IN GENERAL	Pure carbon	Sanctity. Perfection. Fortitude. Pride. Intelligence. Stone of April.

THE RUBY

IN GENERAL	Red corundum	Divine zeal. Human love. Stone of July.

THE EMERALD

IN GENERAL	A green beryl	The victory over the flesh. Spring. Hope. The stone of May.

THE SAPPHIRE

IN GENERAL	Blue corundum	Heavenly truth. Sincerity. Stone of September.

Country	Symbol	Signification
THE PEARL		
IN GENERAL	The secretions of a bivalve covering a grain of sand which has entered the shell	Innocence. Purity. Tears. Stone of St. Margaret.
THE TOPAZ		
IN GENERAL	A heavy silicate, mainly alumina of yellow hue	Fidelity. Fruitfulness. Stone of November.
THE AMETHYST		
IN GENERAL	A quartz of a violet blue color, probably caused by peroxide of iron	Sympathy. Abnegation. Peace. Stone of February.
THE GARNET		
IN GENERAL	A hard red crystal	Deep affection. Stone of January.
THE CARBUNCLE		
IN GENERAL	A precious garnet cut in rounded form	Martyrdom.
THE CRYSTAL		
IN GENERAL	A symmetrical solid, usually transparent, stone	Simplicity. Truthfulness.
THE TURQUOISE		
IN GENERAL	An opaque bluish green stone	Sincere affection. Stone of December.
TURQUOISE MATRIX		
IN GENERAL	Or mother stone which contains the gem	Sincere affection. Stone of December.
THE OPAL		
IN GENERAL	An oxid of silicon, in layers containing water, which takes on prismatic hues	Ancient emblem of good luck. Stone of October.

Country	Symbol	Signification
THE AGATE		
IN GENERAL	A mottled opaque, hard stone of varying shades of browns, greys and dull red	Long life and health. Stone of June.
THE CAT'S EYE		
IN GENERAL	A quartz with fibrous inclusions	Platonic affection.
THE CARNELIAN		
IN GENERAL	A chalcedony of deep, clear red. Sometimes mixed with white	Emblem of distinction.
THE CHRYSOBERYL		
IN GENERAL	Yellowish green or emerald green hard stone	Emblem of patience.
THE BLOODSTONE OR HELIOTROPE		
IN GENERAL	A fibrous green stone streaked with red, with a kidney shaped surface	Mourning. Stone of March. Sacred stone of Babylonians.
THE JASPER		
IN GENERAL	A crypto-crystalline quartz	Pride. Wisdom. Second sight.
THE CORAL		
IN GENERAL	The skeleton of a tiny animal known as the coral polyp	Signifies marriage. Good fortune.
LAPIS LAZULI		
IN GENERAL	A massive oriental stone of rich ultra-marine blue	Nobility.

Country	Symbol	Signification
	THE MOONSTONE	
IN GENERAL	A feldspar containing reflected lights of grey and blue	Thoughtfulness.
	THE ONYX	
IN GENERAL	A stone in two layers of color	Reciprocity.
	THE SARDONYX	
IN GENERAL	Three layers of color	Conjugal fidelity.
	THE LABRADORITE	
IN GENERAL	Spar from Labrador	Subtility. Hidden beauty.
	THE CHRYSOLITE	
IN GENERAL	A silicate of magnesium and iron of yellow hue	Unrequited love.
	AMBER	
IN GENERAL	The gum of extinct pine trees	Tears of the Heliades, who were turned into trees which dropped amber tears on the Greek coast, where the body of their brother Phaeton was washed ashore.
	THE FOUNDATION STONES OF THE NEW JERUSALEM	
	The Jasper, Sapphire, Chalcedony, Emerald, Sardonyx, Sardius, Chrysolite, Beryl, Topaz, Chrysoprase, Jacinth, Amethyst	

FRUITS

"It is by no means true that the ancient systems of mythology have ceased to exist; they have only been diffused and transformed."—*Gubernatis.*

The Rig Veda claims to be the oldest Bible in existence. It is composed of hymns which passed from generation to generation by word of mouth. The locality of the Garden of Eden is claimed by East India.

Country	Symbol	Signification
HEBREW AND PAGAN FORM		
THE APPLE		
JUDEAN	Natural form	Emblem of Eve. The temptation.
SCANDINAVIAN		Emblem of Freya, the northern Venus. Procreation.
GRECIAN		Emblem of Aphrodite, the Grecian Venus. Liberality.
ROMAN	Three golden apples	Symbol of Atalanta as the covetous one.
	Natural form	Emblem of Venus. Symbol of Discordia who threw an apple among wedding guests as revenge for not having been invited to the feast.
		Symbol of the Hesperides Nymphs who guarded the golden apples given by Ge (the Earth) to Hera, the wife of Zeus.
THE PEACH		
CHINESE AND JAPANESE	Natural form	Signifies immortality.
THE QUINCE		
ARABIC AND SPANISH	Natural form	Signifies virility.

Country	Symbol	Signification
THE POMEGRANATE		
EGYPTIAN	Natural form	Signifies fertility. (Because of many seeds.)
PERSIAN, GRECIAN AND ROMAN		Fertility. Abundance. Autumn.
THE PEAR		
CHINESE AND JAPANESE	Natural form	Felicity. Companionship.
THE GRAPE		
GRECIAN	Natural form	Emblem of Dionysus, the wine god.
ROMAN		Emblem of Bacchus. Intoxication.

EARLY CHRISTIAN AND MODERN FORM

Country	Symbol	Signification
APPLES, PEACHES AND PEARS		
IN GENERAL	Natural form	Symbols of the Virgin Mary, as the fruitful one.
	The pear	Emblem of St. Catherine. Felicity.
THE GRAPE		
IN GENERAL	Natural form	Symbol of Christ.
	Cluster of grapes	Unity.
THE POMEGRANATE		
IN GENERAL	Natural form	Emblem of San Juan de Dios as the fertile Christian.
BASKET OF FRUIT		
IN GENERAL	Natural form	Emblem of St. Dorothy.

PLANTS AND BLOSSOMS

"I am a pure lotus, issue of the field of the sun." *Egyptian Book of the Dead—Budge.*

"If thou be born in a poor man's hovel, but hast wisdom, then thou art like the lotus flower growing out of the mud."—*A Buddhist Precept.*

Country	Symbol	Signification
HEBREW AND PAGAN FORM		
THE LOTUS		
EGYPTIAN	As self-fructifying	Emblem of Hapi, god of the Nile. Emblem of Isis.
BUDDHISTIC	Natural or conventional form	Sacred standard of the gods. Universal Matrix or mother. Emblem of Buddha, as the enlightened, and the "Jewel in the Lotus."
THE PAPYRUS		
EGYPTIAN	When on sceptre	Sacred standard of youth, vigor and learning.
HOMA AND SOMA PLANTS		
PERSIAN AND HINDU	The extracted juice which is taken as a beverage	Elixir of the gods, giving eternal life.
THE TREE PEONY		
CHINESE	Natural or conventional form	Royal flower.
JAPANESE		Emblem of dignity.
THE REED		
CHINESE AND JAPANESE	Natural form	Learning.
PLUM BLOSSOMS		
JAPANESE	Natural or conventional form	Womanly purity. Emblem of winter.

Country	Symbol	Signification
	CHERRY BLOSSOMS	
JAPANESE	Natural or conventional form	Womanly beauty. Emblem of spring.
	THE AZALEA	
JAPANESE	Natural form	The garden beauty. Flower of April.
	THE WISTARIA	
JAPANESE	Natural form	Vine of Happiness. "Plant of a thousand years."
	THE PAULOWNIA	
JAPANESE	Natural form	Emblem of the Emperor. Rectitude.
	THE MAGNOLIA	
JAPANESE	Natural form	Flower of May.
	THE IRIS	
JAPANESE	When purple	Signifies mourning.
	When not purple	The betrothal flower. Emblem of June.
	THE MORNING GLORY	
JAPANESE	Natural form	Flower of July.
	THE CHRYSANTHEMUM	
JAPANESE	Natural form	The Imperial pride. Flower of October.
	THE TEA PLANT AND FLOWER	
JAPANESE	Natural form	Rank and riches.
	THE ROSE	
MOHAMMEDAN	Natural form	Emblem of Mohammed's eyes. Flower of Iran.

Country	Symbol	Signification
THE TULIP		
MOHAMMEDAN	Natural form	Ardent affection.
THE VINE		
GRECIAN	Natural form	Emblem of Dionysus, god of wine.
ROMAN		Emblem of Bacchus, god of wine.
PERSIAN		Joy of living. Wisdom of materiality.
CARNATION		
PERSIAN	Natural form	Emblem of Persia.
THE ALMOND FLOWER		
JUDEAN	Natural form	Emblem of Aaron.
WHEAT EARS		
GRECIAN	Natural form	Emblem of Demeter, goddess of agriculture.
ROMAN		Emblem of Ceres, goddess of the harvest.
POPPY		
ROMAN	Natural form	Sleep, emblem of Circe.

EARLY CHRISTIAN AND MODERN FORM
THE ROSE

Country	Symbol	Signification
IN GENERAL	Natural form	Emblem of the Virgin. Erythaean Sibyl. Signifies human love in modern thought.
	Crown of roses	Symbol of St. Elizabeth of Hungary.
ENGLISH	The red rose	Flower of England. Flower of the Yorkists. (Device of the War of the Roses.)
	The white rose	Flower of the Lancastrians.

Country	Symbol	Signification
THE LILY		
IN GENERAL	Natural form	Emblem of the Virgin. Gabriel as the angel of the Annunciation. St. Francis as representing chastity.
	Fleur de lis or flag lily	Emblem of St. Louis. France. The Medici of Florence.
	The iris	Messenger of good news.
GERANIUM		
IN GENERAL	Natural form	Conjugal affection.
THE NARCISSUS		
IN GENERAL	Natural form	Grace. Self-consciousness.
THE EGLANTINE		
IN GENERAL	Natural form	Signifies poetry. Elegance; "to the manner born."
THE HELIOTROPE		
IN GENERAL	Natural form	Devotion. Zeal. Strength in sweetness.
THE HIBISCUS		
IN GENERAL	Natural form	Frailty. Conservativeness.
THE HYACINTH		
IN GENERAL	Natural form	High estate. Pride. Exclusiveness.
THE JONQUIL		
IN GENERAL	Natural form	Vanity. Imprudence. Uncontrolled affection.
THE HYDRANGEA		
IN GENERAL	Natural form	Coldness. Frigidity. Massive beauty.
THE VIOLET		
IN GENERAL	Natural form	Modesty. Sweetness. Loyalty.

Country	Symbol	Signification
THE LILAC		
IN GENERAL	Natural form	First emotions of love.
THE MAGNOLIA		
IN GENERAL	Natural form	Dignity. Respectability.
THE MARGUERITE		
IN GENERAL	Natural form	Preference in love.
THE SNOW DROP		
IN GENERAL	Natural form	Purity of heart.
THE FORGET-ME-NOT		
IN GENERAL	Natural form	True love.
THE IVY		
IN GENERAL	Natural form	Longevity. Dependence. Despondency.
THE CLEMATIS		
IN GENERAL	Natural form	Gladness. Upward flight.
THE BALSAM		
IN GENERAL	Natural form	The zealous benefactor. The Samaritan flower.
ORANGE BLOSSOMS		
IN GENERAL	Natural form	Fruitfulness. Exuberance. Flower of the bride.
THE MARIGOLD		
IN GENERAL	Natural form	Emblem of the Virgin as Mary's gold. Worth.
THE CORN FLOWER		
GERMAN	Natural form	National flower of Prussia. Emblem of Queen Louise.

Country	Symbol	Signification
	THE SHAMROCK	
IRISH	Natural form	National flower of Ireland. Emblem of St. Patrick. The triad leaf.
	THE THISTLE	
SCOTCH	Natural form	Flower of Scotland. Guardian of the race.
	THE HEATHER	
SCOTCH	Natural form	Flower of the Scottish clans. Sympathy. Allegiance.
	THE EDELWEISS	
SWISS	Natural form	Flower of the Alps. Chastity.
	THE GRAPE VINE	
IN GENERAL	Natural form	Emblem of Jesus who said, "I am the vine."
	THE WHEAT	
IN GENERAL	Natural form	Staff of life. Prosperity.
	The ears of wheat	Emblem of Ruth as model of constancy.
	Stack of wheat	Body of Christ.

UNCLASSIFIED SYMBOLS

"A symbol is either representative, indicates a thing and makes you think of it, as a bunch of grapes over a house door indicating wine, is called a public house sign; or it is vicarious, as a five pound note stands for five sovereigns. The bunch of grapes reminds you of the juice of the vine but you can't drink it. The piece of paper passes vicariously for five pieces of gold and you can spend it."—*Rev. R. St. John Tyrwhitt.*

Country	Symbol	Signification
	HEBREW AND PAGAN FORM	
	THE SISTRUM	
EGYPTIAN	An instrument used by priestesses during ritual, shaped like a half circle drawn together at the end and crossed by loose bars of metal which jingle when shaken. This is fastened to a handle which is shaped like the Tau cross	Chastity.
JAPANESE	Instrument used by priestesses in the Shinto ritual. It has the form of a wand encircled by small bells and is shaken to attract the attention of the gods.	Virtue and piety.
	THE HAND	
JUDEAN	Natural form	Might. Justice. The Almighty.
	With first three fingers extended and thumb and little finger closed on the palm	Was, Is and Is to Come.
BUDDHISTIC	One finger and thumb touching each other	Perfect action of thought with his perfect plan.

Country	Symbol	Signification
THE HAND—CONTINUED		
MOHAMMEDAN	Usually held upright, fingers and thumb extended	Emblem of Mohammed. Signifying power. Of his daughter, Fatima, signifying prosperity and long life.
ROMAN	Thumbs of Vestals turned up	Mercy to vanquished.
	Thumbs of Vestals turned down (in the arena)	Death to vanquished.
CHINESE AND JAPANESE	A many handed deity called Kwannon	Mercy. Contemplation.
THE TRIPOD		
GRECIAN	Usual form	Emblem of Delphic Oracle. The three mysteries.
THE ARK		
JUDEAN	Usual form	Signifies the deluge. Emblem of Noah. The covenant of the Jews with Jehovah.
WATER		
EGYPTIAN	Natural or hieroglyphic form	The passive principle. The Nile. Fertility. The river Styx which leads to Hades.
CHINESE	Water fall	Signifies humility.
JAPANESE	Primary water fall	Signifies the masculine principle.
	The secondary water fall	Feminine principle.
THE VEIL		
PHOENICIAN	Usual form	Emblem of Tanit, goddess of beauty.
IN GENERAL	Dotted with stars	Emblem of Night.
THE UMBRELLA		
EGYPTIAN	When held over the head	Emblem of honorable distinction.
CHINESE	When held over the head	Protection of the throne.

Country	Symbol	Signification
	THE STAFF AND ROD	
BUDDHISTIC	With jingling rings attached to a rod and carried by the pilgrims: to disperse insects and small animals without injuring them	Kindness. Mercy.
GRECIAN	Thyrsus or staff twined with ivy and tipped with a pine cone	Sceptre of Dionysus, god of fertility.
BABYLONIAN	Hazel guiding rods	Divination.
ROMAN	Wand tipped by a globe which is surmounted by an eagle	Emblem of Jove. The Roman Legions.
	Budded staff	Emblem of Hellespontine Sibyl.
JAPANESE	Tokko or one spoke of wheel of the law	The irresistible power of prayer.
EGYPTIAN	Staff in the shape of a crook	Sovereignty.
	The lotus sceptre	Virility.
	The papyrus sceptre	Eternal youth.
SCANDINAVIAN	Staff with circle, used as sceptre	The sun's rays. Divine light.
	THE HAMMER	
GRECIAN	Usual form	Emblem of Hephaestus, the divine forger.
SCANDINAVIAN	When shaped like a Tau cross	Emblem of Thor as god of thunder and lightning.
JAPANESE	Usual form	Daikoku as god of wealth which is taken from the earth.
	THE CLUB	
HINDU	Usual form	Emblem of Yama as judge of the Unseen.
ROMAN	When knotted	Symbol of Hercules, god of strength.

Country	Symbol	Signification
THE CLUB—CONTINUED		
CHINESE AND JAPANESE	Club or mace with heart shaped head resembling the sacred fungus which grows at the foot of Buddha's tree	Divine office.
WHIP OR SCOURGE		
EGYPTIAN	Club or stick with lashes	Sovereignty by force.
	The club shaped as a flail	Emblem of guardian diety of agriculture.
THE BOOK		
GRECIAN AND ROMAN	When sealed	Chastity.
	Either closed or open	Emblem of Cumaean Sibyl who prophesied and wrote the laws of civil and religious Rome.
THE BALL		
EGYPTIAN	Usual form	Emblem of the sun and the moon.
CHINESE AND JAPANESE		The omnipotent pearl of wisdom or Hoshu-no-tama.
THE FAN		
JAPANESE	War fan	Signal ensign.
	Tea ceremony fan of three sticks	The charm of simplicity.
THE BUCKET, BAG OR BASKET		
EGYPTIAN	Which holds sanctified water for the tree of life and the souls of men	Divine refreshment.
EARTH AND WATER		
PERSIAN	When used together as offerings	Subjection to the crown.

Country	Symbol	Signification
	THE RING	
TEUTONIC	Usual form	Emblem of promise. Emblem of the Rhine daughters of the Nibelungenlied.
	THE GOHEI	
JAPANESE	Paper strips representing cloth	The fruit of the loom. Sacred offering to Shinto gods.
	THE MIRROR	
PHOENICIAN	Usual form	Emblem of Istar, goddess of beauty.
JAPANESE	When in a Shinto temple	Emblem of Amaterasu as leading goddess of the Shinto faith, signifying truth.
GRECIAN AND ROMAN	Usual form	Emblem of truth.
	THE FEET	
EGYPTIAN AND GRECIAN	A winged foot crushing a butterfly	Emblem of Serapis, the Greek deity, which was the Egyptian bull Apis, worshipped after his death, in Greece.
EAST INDIAN	Footprints showing triscula or swastica	Emblem of Buddha's pilgrimage and service.
	FIRE	
EGYPTIAN	In the abstract	The active principle.
PERSIAN		Life of the soul.
JAPANESE		Emblem of Fudo, as signifying fire of wisdom.
GRECIAN	Symbol of Prometheus, who stole celestial fire and gave it to mankind.	
SCANDINAVIAN		Residence of Muspel, genius of fire.
	CIRCLE OF FIRE	
IN GENERAL	Usual form	Inviolability. Chastity. Magic.
TEUTONIC		Symbol of Brunhilde.

Country	Symbol	Signification
	THE PIPES	
GRECIAN AND ROMAN	Usual form	Emblem of woodland deities, who evoked the harmony of Nature. Symbol of Pan.
ANCIENT SCOTCH AND CELTS	The bagpipes	The voice of the clans.
	THE CUP OR BEAKER	
EGYPTIAN AND ASSYRIAN	When used as libation vessel	Signifies renewed spiritual vigor.
PERSIAN	When seven ringed, symbolizing the seven heavens	Emblem of Jamshyd, the king.
JUDEAN	In chalice or goblet form	Emblem of Solomon.
GRECIAN	Usual form	Emblem of Ganymede, cup bearer to Zeus.
ROMAN		Emblem of Hebe, handmaiden of Jupiter.
SCANDINAVIAN		Signifies the mead drank at the table of the gods.
	THE MASK	
JAPANESE	Usual form	Signifies the No dance sacred to the gods.
ROMAN		Symbol of Thalia, muse of comedy. Dissimulation.
NORTH AMERICAN INDIAN		Protection against evil spirits. A scare devil.
	THE EGG	
EGYPTIAN (COPTIC)	Usual form	Signifies creation.
EAST INDIAN, CHINESE AND JAPANESE		Signifies the Universe.

Country	Symbol	Signification
	THE TOMB OR TOMB STONE	
ANCIENT TRIBES	Usual form	Residence of the dead. Finger post of the soul.
JAPANESE	Sotoba or tomb stone of the Fujiwara clan	The five elements: ether, air, fire, water, earth.
	THE VASE	
EGYPTIAN	Three large vases	Signifies the Nile river.
GRECIAN	Amphora or vase of two handles	Blessing of wine or grain.
	Hydria, a pitcher vase	Blessing of water.
	THE EYE	
EGYPTIAN	One eye	Emblem of Osiris, the sun god.
	Two eyes, one black, the other white	Emblem of Horus as the night and day and the perfect grain.
ASSYRIAN	Natural form	Emblem of the sun and moon.
	THE DEW	
ORIENTAL	Usual form	Emblem of delicacy. Fragility.
SCANDINAVIAN	The honeydew	Emblem of goddess Servitur, who drops honey from Yggdrasil or tree of life upon those deserving benefaction.
	THE BELL	
BURMESE	Temple wind bells	Music of the gods.
CHINESE AND JAPANESE	Evening temple bells	Prayers to the gods.
	THE COMB	
PICTISH	Usual form	The sun's rays. Emblem of Venus.
	THE SAIL	
EGYPTIAN	Usual form	The breath.

Country	Symbol	Signification
	THE LADDER	
JUDEAN	Usual form	Emblem of Jacob.
EGYPTIAN		Emblem of Set who climbs to Heaven's palace.
	THE LOOM	
IN GENERAL	Usual form	Industry.
GRECIAN		Emblem of Penelope the faithful.
	RICE BALES	
JAPANESE	Usual form	Emblem of Daikoku, god of wealth and rice.
	THE BOAT	
EGYPTIAN	Usual form	Signifies bark of the sun. Bark of Charon the boatman who takes souls across the river Styx to Hades. Bark of the Elysian Fields.
	THE HORN	
JUDEAN	On head of Moses	Truth and Justice.
BABYLONIAN	On head of Bel, the chief god	Material strength.
GRECIAN	Usual form	Emblem of Bacchus. Alexander the Great called the "Two horned power."
SCANDINAVIAN		Hospitality. Measure of joy.
	MUSICAL INSTRUMENTS	
JUDEAN	The harp	Contemplation. Symbol of David, who charmed the king.
GRECIAN		National instrument of poetic song.
EGYPTIAN	The lyre	Harmony of the gods.
HEBREW		The constellation Vega the lyre.
EGYPTIAN	The lute	Emblem of Nefer-Hetep—lord of joy.
EARLY FRENCH AND SPANISH		Emblem of the Troubadour.

Country	Symbol	Signification
	THE CLOUD	
CHINESE	Cloud banks	Immortality.
PERSIAN	Rising smoke	Joys of the weed. Retrospection.
JUDEAN	Frankincense clouds	Emblem of race of Japhet.
	Myrrh clouds	Sacred to race of Ham.
	THE APRON	
EGYPTIAN	Usual form	Royalty.
	THE PADLOCK	
CHINESE	When worn as an amulet	Long life. Prosperity.

UNCLASSIFIED OBJECTS

"By outward forms early Christians were inspired with feelings of devotion and love and in the absence of books, derived from them their chief knowledge of sacred things. To the unlearned, they spoke a clear and intelligible language: that they were full of meaning and poetry, no one who will endeavor to interpret them can doubt."—*Louisa Twining.*

Country	Symbol	Signification
	EARLY CHRISTIAN AND MODERN FORM	
	THE STAFF AND ROD	
IN GENERAL	Pastoral staff (Crozier)	Religious jurisdiction.
	With gourd	Signifies the Archangel Raphael as a pilgrim.
	Usual form	Emblem of old age.
	Represented by bread	The staff of life.
	With leaves and dates	Symbol of St. Christopher, patron of travelers.
	The rod	Symbol of the Creator who comforts.
	Flowering rod	Symbol of Aaron, the priest, and Joseph, the successful suitor.
	THE HAND	
IN GENERAL	When in clouds	The first Person of the Trinity.
	When holding lightning bolts or emitting rays of light	The first Person of the Trinity.
	Usual form	Emblem of the Tibertine Sibyl.
	With first two fingers and thumb extended and third and fourth closed on palm	The Trinity.

Country	Symbol	Signification
	THE HEART	
IN GENERAL	Natural or conventional form	Piety, Love.
	When pierced by an arrow	Charity.
	THE ANCHOR	
IN GENERAL	Usual form	Hope. Emblem of St. Nicholas, patron of Russia.
	THE SCALES	
IN GENERAL	Usual form	Justice. Symbol of St. Michael as Captain of the Heavenly Hosts.
	THE CENSER	
IN GENERAL	When burning	Piety before men.
	EMBLEMS OF THE PASSION	
IN GENERAL	Cross, nails, thorns, hammer, reed, scourge, purse and dice	The Crucifixion.
	WINGS	
IN GENERAL	Bat's wings	Emblem of Lucifer.
	When spread	Aspiration. Translation.
	Usual form	Protection. Ambition. Astronomy. Night.
	THE HAIR	
IN GENERAL	When flowing	Symbol of Mary Magdalen as the penitent.
	When covering like a garment	Symbol of St. Agnes, who, when persecuted, prayed for clothing. The glory of a woman.
	WATER	
IN GENERAL	In a font The Jordan river	Signifies baptism
	When gushing from a rock	Emblem of Moses.

Country	Symbol	Signification
	THE WEB	
IN GENERAL	Usual form	Destiny. Energy. Industry of the Christian at work about his Father's business.
	THE UMBRELLA	
ITALIAN	When held over the head of a dignitary	Honor. Position.
	THE SNOOD	
ANCIENT SCOTCH	A band of cloth, ribbon or metal, entirely circling the head	Signifies virginity.
	THE SHELL	
IN GENERAL	Usual form	Pilgrimage. Emblem of St. James the elder.
	THE SHIP	
IN GENERAL	When held in the hand	Signifies the Church.
	Usual form	The greyhound of the sea.
	THE RIVER	
IN GENERAL	Usual form	Signifies life.
	THE KNIFE	
IN GENERAL	Sacrificial knife	Symbol of Zadkiel, who stayed the hand of Abraham. Emblem of St. Bartholomew, the instrument of his martyrdom.
	THE GRIDIRON	
IN GENERAL	Usual form	Emblem of St. Lawrence, the instrument of his martyrdom.
	THE RING	
IN GENERAL	When held in hand of representations of the Christ Child	Symbol of St. Catherine in her mystical marriage with Christ.
	Usual form	The symbol of marriage.
	SKULL AND CROSS BONES	
IN GENERAL	Usual form	Brevity of human life.

Country	Symbol	Signification
	THE ORGAN	
IN GENERAL	Usual form	Symbol of St. Cecelia, legendary inventor of the organ.
	THE CORNUCOPIA	
IN GENERAL	Usual form	Abundance. The harvest.
	THE CUP	
IN GENERAL	When covered with a wafer	The Eucharist.
	Cup with serpent	Symbol of St. John, indicating immunity from poison.
	Shedding rays of light	The Holy Grail or cup containing the blood of Christ, caught at the Crucifixion, by Joseph of Arimathaea.
	Usual form	Symbol of St. Benedict. St. Donato. Bitterness. Sorrow. Joy. Happiness.
	With handles to pass from hand to hand, known as "The loving cup"	Brotherly love.
	THE HORN	
IN GENERAL	Usual form	Emblem of Roland, the Paladin of Charlemagne. Plenty.
	The left hand corner of the front of an altar	The gospel horn.
	The right hand corner of the front of an altar.	The epistle horn.
	"The little end of the horn"	Loss. Grief.
	THE BEE HIVE	
IN GENERAL	Usual form	Symbol of St. Bernard and St. Ambrose. Industry. System.
	THE GARMENT	
IN GENERAL	Mantle or cloak	Charity.

Country	Symbol	Signification
	THE GARMENT—CONTINUED	
IN GENERAL	When dividing with a beggar	Symbol of St. Martin.
	MONASTIC HABITS	
IN GENERAL	Black cassock and square cap	Order of the Jesuits.
	White habit, black mantle with hood	Order of the Dominicans.
	Dark brown habit, white mantle	Order of the Carmelites.
	Brown or gray habit, fastened about waist with a knotted rope	Order of the Franciscans.
	THE APRON	
IN GENERAL	Usual form	Service. Masonic emblem of ancient craft.
	THE FACE	
IN GENERAL	Face or head of an angel or cherub	Emblem of St. Matthew, who wrote the genealogy of Christ.
	FUR	
IN GENERAL	Ermine	Emblem of royalty.
HERALDIC, ENGLISH	Pean or black and yellow furs, mixed	Honour.
	Ermine	Honour.
	Vair or blue and white furs, mixed	Honour.
	THE NAPKIN	
IN GENERAL	When showing portrait of Jesus	Emblem of St. Veronica, who wiped the perspiration from the Saviour's face, when He was carrying the cross. (Legendary.)

Country	Symbol	Signification
	THE BOX OR VASE OR DISH	
IN GENERAL	When of alabaster	Emblem of Mary Magdalen.
	Dish holding eyes	Emblem of Santa Lucia, who removed her eyes and sent them to a presumptuous suitor. (Legendary.)
	TIME	
IN GENERAL	The hour glass	Measuring of time.
	The scythe	The instrument of time.
	The sun dial	Nature's clock.
	THE CRADLE	
IN GENERAL	Usual form	Emblem of Nativity. The Samian Sibyl, who prophesied the Nativity.
	THE KEY	
IN GENERAL	Keys held in the hand	Symbol of St. Peter as holding keys of heaven.
	When at girdle	St. Martha the housekeeper.
	THE TABLET	
IN GENERAL	When of stone	Signifies the Ten Commandments.
	When connected with compass and square	Signifies geometry.
	THE HAMMER AND CHISEL	
IN GENERAL	Usual form	Signifies sculpture and the crafts.
	PALETTE AND BRUSHES	
IN GENERAL	Usual form	Signifies painting.
	SCROLL	
IN GENERAL	With pencil or quill pen	Signifies literature.
	Scroll with harp	Signifies music.

Country	Symbol	Signification
	THE BELL	
IN GENERAL	Usual form	The preacher.
	The vesper bell	Evening prayer.
	The passing bell	Dissolution. Tolling years.
	Curfew bell	Forced retirement.
	THE ROCK	
IN GENERAL	Usual form	Emblem of Peter. Truth.
	THE BALL	
IN GENERAL	Usual form	Emblem of St. Nicholas.
	Three balls	Emblem of pawn broker.
	Balls	Cognizance of the Medici banking house of Tuscany.
	THE GLOBE	
IN GENERAL	Usual form	Rhetoric.
	With cross	Emblem of church and state. Dominion.
ENGLISH	Globe with dove	Ruler by divine right.
	THE BOOK	
IN GENERAL	When closed	Knowledge.
	When open	Perfect knowledge.
	With roll	Emblem of Uriel as light of knowledge.

BIBLIOGRAPHY

1. The works of James Fergusson, F.R.S.
2. *The Gods of the Egyptians*—E. A. T. W. Budge.
3. *The Grammar of the Lotus*—W. H. Goodyear, M.A.
4. *Buddha*—Dr. Herman Oldenberg.
5. *Chinese Ancient Symbolism*—Joseph Edkins, D.D.
6. *The Origins of Pictish Symbolism*—The Earl of Southesk, K.T.
7. *The Migration of Symbols*—Goblet d'Alviella.
8. *The Buddhist Praying Wheel*—William Simpson.
9. *Dictionnare des Symboles*—P. Verneuil.
10. *Hindu Mythology*—W. J. Wilkins.
11. *The Rubaiyat of Omar Khayyam.*
12. *The History of Arabia*—Andrew Crichton.
13. *Ancient Arabian Poetry*—C. J. Lyall, M.A.
14. *Symbolism of the East and West*—Murray-Aynsley.
15. *Architecture, Mysticism and Myth*—W. R. Lethaby.
16. *Ideal Metrology*—Herman Gaylord.
17. *Ceramic Art in Remote Ages*—J. B. Waring.
18: *Demonology*—Sir Walter Scott.
19. *Ko-ji-ki*—Translated by D. H. Chamberlain.
20. *The Canon*, with a Preface—R. B. Cunninghame.
21. *The Night of the Gods*—John O'Neil.
22. *The Hymns of the Rig Veda*—R. T. H. Griffith.
23. *Scandinavian Mythology* (*The Eddas*)—Grenville Pigott.
24. *Horns of Honour*—F. T. Elworthy.
25. *Symbolism in Art*—F. E. Hulme.
26. *Völsunga Saga*—Translated by William Morris.
27. *The Mabinogian* (from *Popular Studies in Myth*)—Ivor B. John, M.A.
28. *Landscape Gardening in Japan*—Josiah Conder.
29. *Mediaeval German Epics*—G. T. Dippold, Ph.D.
30. *Studies of the Greek Poets*—John A. Symonds.

31. *Artistic Japan*—Compiled by Bing.

32. *Ecclesiastical Ornament*—A. W. Pugin.

33. *The Symbolisms of Heraldry*—W. Cecil Wade.

34. *Christian Art and Symbolism*—Rev. R. St. John Tyrwhitt.

35. *Colour* (in *Quarterly Papers on Architecture*)— T. Inman.

36. *Early Christian Symbolism*—J. R. Allen, F.S.A.

37. *Popular Poetry of the Finns*—C. J. Bilson, M.A.

38. *The Sibylline Oracles*—Sir John Floyer.

39. *The Best Book of All*—F. J. Hamilton, D.D.

40. Books of Genesis, Exodus, Leviticus, Chronicles, Samuel, Isaiah, Jeremiah, Ezekiel, St. Luke, St. John, Revelation.

GENERAL INDEX